PETER COOK

Architectural Monographs No 28

PETER COOK
SIX CONVERSATIONS

A.D. ACADEMY EDITIONS • **E&S** ERNST & SOHN

Architectural Monographs No 28
Editorial Offices
42 Leinster Gardens London W2 3AN

Editorial and Design Team: Andrea Bettella (Senior Designer),
Owen Thomas (Design); Nicola Hodges, Lucy Trentham (Editorial)

Photographic Credits
p68, p69 photographs courtesy of Waltraud Krase

Cover: Finchley Road 2, 1992
Frontis: Staedelschule, Frankfurt, Canteen (Peter Cook, Christine Hawley
and Klaus Bollinger), 1992

First published in Great Britain in 1993 by
ACADEMY EDITIONS
An imprint of Academy Group Ltd

ACADEMY GROUP LTD
42 Leinster Gardens London W2 3AN
ERNST & SOHN
Hohenzollerndamm 170, 1000 Berlin 31
Members of the VCH Publishing Group

ISBN 1 85490 152 4 (HB)
ISBN 1 85490 156 7 (PB)

Distributed in the United States of America in 1993 by
ST MARTIN'S PRESS
175 Fifth Avenue, New York, NY 10012

Printed and bound in Singapore

CONTENTS

SIX CONVERSATIONS

The basic 1992 lecture: first given on January 2, 1992 for the Tenth Anniversary celebration of the 'Sadna' school of Design in Tel Aviv, developed for Copenhagen, Lund, Oslo and Aarhus in Spring 1992, revised July 1992.

I am holding six conversations with myself . . . or six preoccupations which carry on over time and around which I find myself working. They don't run chronologically and I don't become obsessed by one preoccupation only to abandon it totally. It comes back again and again and is layered into the others. Something that interested me ten years ago is still there in the recesses of my mind and will return in some aspect of a new piece of work. Even to separate them here is very artificial.

CONVERSATION 1
MODESTY, FUN AND THE ELLIPTICAL ENGLISH METHOD

Not a *direct* method, you will note, but an *elliptical* method. Which is an ironic preoccupation, since I spend so much of my time in countries (Germany, the USA, Israel) where directness and definitiveness are honoured. This is paralleled in my relationship with architectural friends, which rarely consists of a head-on discussion of positions or icons. It is elliptical – considering a number of positions and *possibilities* and retaining the right to harden up the definitions at the least likely moment; the right to scramble the sets of values; the right to introduce totally non-architectural anecdotes; the right to hold an ambiguous position that is not necessarily disclosed, but perhaps unearthed by one's friends, bit by bit.

English phenomena, particularly those that are found in parks and gardens, fit the attitude perfectly. In the picture of a little wooden seat under a tree there is nothing apparently grand or heroic. It is quite modest, certainly small and not expensive. But look more closely at it, imagine its likely context and its degree of finesse. Almost certainly it faces a prospect of several hundred metres and was commissioned by someone with power and influence. Beware of its apparent modesty: in the same way, beware of the apparent modesty and shyness of the English conversation . . . the layers conceal an arrogance of assurance and that the values can be shrugged at suggests anything but weakness. The Anglo-Saxon schools of architecture enjoy the 'crit' process – where the teacher will invite all sorts of people to join in and even criticise the methods of their host. If it is a good one, it will be difficult for you to know whether the critics really *liked* or *hated* the work. The conversation will have moved around and above and

Garden Seat, Rousham
A Student 'Jury'
Pleasure grounds, Blackpool in the 1960s

below the pragmatics of the drawn object. Many students from other cultures are confused by this. In Germany the professor will never invite outsiders and will declaim 'this is impossible' . . . 'this is correct' and his assistants will twitter nervously. If we are being pedagogic, which in my terms means encouraging, we will say 'that is quite *interesting* . . . and *maybe* and perhaps . . . and it could . . . ' The collage of hints and observations are very much the collage of thoughts that one has when designing. So someone will say, 'What if?' and the other, 'What if not?' I am suggesting that value systems are only staging-posts . . . they are only go-betweens on the same level as the photographer, the transcriber, the performer.

I come from the seaside. A place where much more is tolerated than in the normal English town or village. In an old picture from the 1970s, a kiosk is offering candyfloss. But if you know the English eating scene, you will know that this kiosk is a replica of the plastic tomato from which you squeeze tomato ketchup. But it is yellow. So you have to ask yourself, 'Why is something that is selling candyfloss, and was probably built to sell icecream, there in the shape of a tomato (not a real tomato but a plastic tomato) and is not (anyway) the right colour?' I would rather spend time thinking this one out intellectually than fussing around Perugia.

The 'House in the Clouds' at Thorpeness is a similar case. The house part is in a funny place. In fact the house part is not a house but was built as a water tank, and the part underneath as the house. Except that this is no longer true . . . for the community no longer needed the tank and they came in with the oxyaceteline burners and put a house back into the tank. Sort it out in your mind, this is a culture that is desperate to rediscover values and criteria in architecture!

'House in the Clouds', Thorpeness

I like things of this ilk and was therefore quite ready to respond when the Leo Castelli Gallery had its 'Follies' show. The 'Lantern from Secret Blue' is almost certainly near to the sea, and located a short distance from the house and almost certainly viewable from the terrace. 'How lovely, a sweet little white tower,' murmurs the weekend visitor. 'I'm sure you get a marvellous view of the sea . . . ' But if the visitor can be persuaded to walk down to the tower, into the tower and climb slowly up to experience the total surround of blue – a strong Klein-like blue – and clutch onto the ever-more eccentric profile of the handrail, he (or she) will of course emerge and, yes, have a perfect view of the sea. The spookiness of the inside against the blandness of the outside has to be read against the issues of assumption and discovery, obviousness and actuality . . . I can't stand the full frontal approach to architecture, which is why I found Post-Modernism such a yawn.

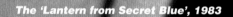

The 'Lantern from Secret Blue', 1983

A LANTERN FROM SECRET BLUE

If architecture is also a question of cause and effect, it helps to have a sense of humour. Christine Hawley and I were asked to design a structure in the tradition of the Japanese 'Yatai' or mobile shop (for the Nagoya Exposition of 1990), and our task was to display imported fabrics. We felt that the purely sideways-on condition was too boring and so we designed a three-dimensional cage up which you could climb and pass in amongst the hung fabrics. We were flown from London to see the Yatai in action . . . a giant tea cosy! So much effort had gone towards the making of something that had (for us) hilarious connotations even though it fulfilled the brief. Strip away the hangings and you get quite an architectonic object, of course. And this all points at the hermetic nature of architectural observation and 'correct' taste: who is to say that a tea-cosy is a ridiculous object ?

'Yatai', moveable shop, Nagoya (Cook & Hawley)

Indeed, I have always had a taste for things that are 'globby'. My ideal comic caption might not be 'Wizzz' or 'Zapp' but '*Plooosh*' and its attendant actions of '*Slurping*' or wrapping. In projects such as 'Gunge' one uses a considerable quantity of cement slurry, a few odd nails, a bit of plaster, keep squeezing it in ('Plooosh . . . Plooosh') and don't expect it to look like anything.

'*Gunge*'

for incision

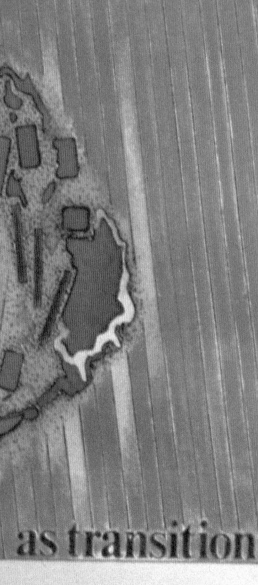

as transition

Right back in the early Archigram
days, the notion was that the existing
vocabulary of architecture was a
product of the philosophies of
Buckminster Fuller or Paolozzi, so it is
little wonder that when one is making
architectural compositions they are
composite as well as composed . . .
both slurped and straight . . . OM
Ungers meeting tomato ketchup at
least halfway.

So both arrogance and modesty
exist together in the English method;
when making fun one is at one's most
serious and the elliptical method
enables the condition to be constantly moving . . . constantly under
scrutiny. Even if my use of the word
'elliptical' is consciously borrowed
from John Hejduk. You have to notice
that the elliptical curve is one in
which the speed increases and then
decreases imperceptibly.

Montreal Tower, 1963

CONVERSATION 2
METAMORPHOSIS

My next theme is that of *metamorphosis*, which isn't simple change – but to do with it. As I was brought up by the seaside, my claim for a natural response to the idea of metamorphosis is simply that the town has to absorb many more people in the summer and its elements metamorphose. In March and April, people start to unwrap things and pull pieces of electrical cable out and start screwing things and building things. A town that was tight and folded (and rather good) in the winter – far more deliciously sinister than in summer – begins to unfold. All the people arrive and it's all very silly and jolly. Then, by September and October it starts to fall, the wind blows and it all slowly fo[lds] up. A metamorphic process. One begins to think: Why don't cities [do] this more? Why can't they meta[mor]phose? Why do they have to be [so] tight? Why can't our architect[ure] respond to circumstances? S[u]ch a conversation became centra[l] to Archigram discussions: prompted by our friend, Cedric Price, and maybe by the seaside origins of another Archigram man, Dennis Crompton, who comes from Blackpool.

One of my favourite metamorphic conditions is the coastal marshland, where the water will insidiously creep amongst the mud and the growths and then go again. Is it land or is it sea? I love that, I love its ambiguity. Is it land or is it sea? And at what point does it become land and at what *point* does it become sea? A marvellous model for an urban condition. I am constantly fascinated by the soft edge, the double-action condition, the melting of the city into the suburban condition and the melting of *it* into the countryside. In this sense, the English 'Every city is a village' tradition is lurking there all the time.

Many years ago, I took that English suburb that we all are conditioned to hate, and started a story line about architectural interference. I called it 'ADDHOX', because the interferences were certainly ad hoc. The essential process of such a project is thus: one starts with the first stage and the second well in mind, but with only a hazy idea of the third. By the time of the fourth, an idea of the fifth . . . but the sixth is hazy. Suddenly, the ultimate stage (in this case, a heady, crazy situation) is suggested by the pull of the project itself. 'Stop! Stop!' it cries, 'enough is enough.'

So it is as if the project carries you along with it, having a spirit and force of its own. Sometimes you really don't know where it is going to go. So I am not quite sure which stage of the sequence is my favourite or is most typical – and that's the point about metamorphosis: it is all equally relevant, in an equally finished or unfinished state.

Addhox Sequence, 1971

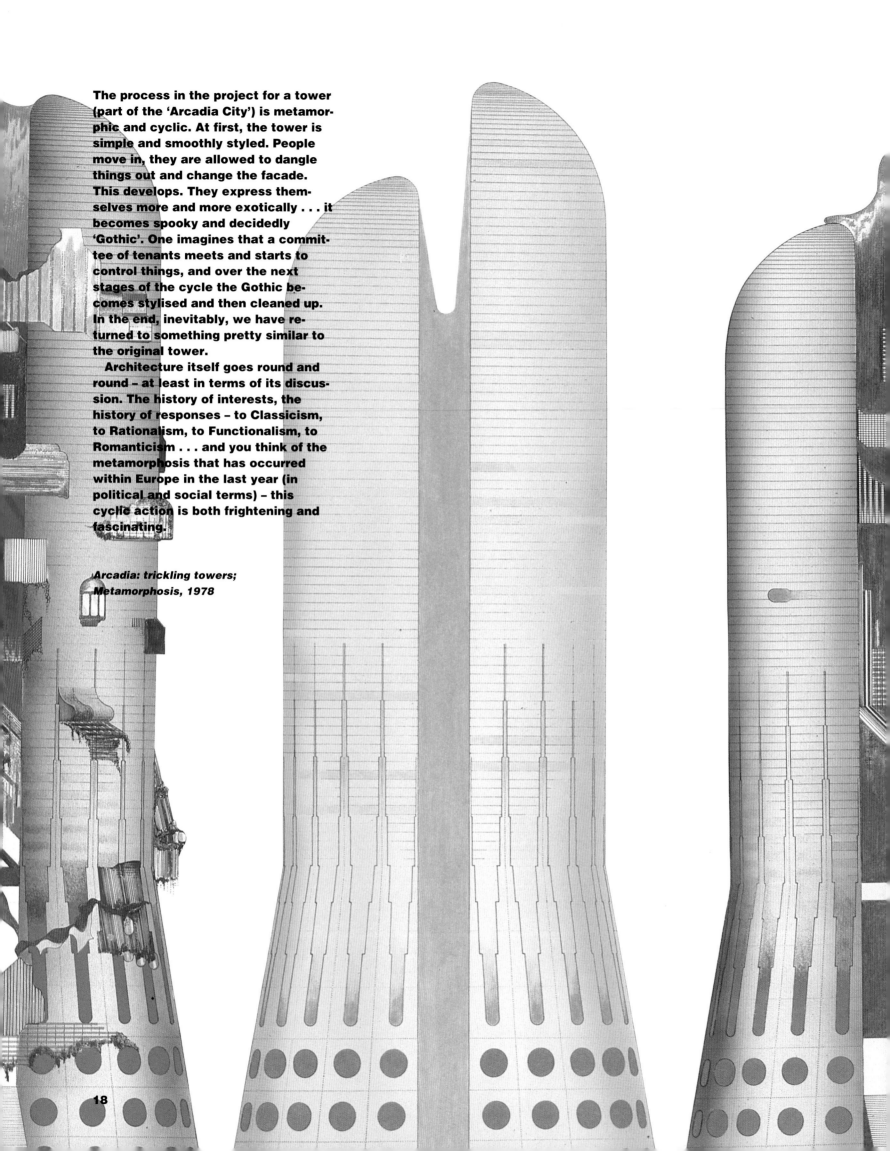

The process in the project for a tower (part of the 'Arcadia City') is metamorphic and cyclic. At first, the tower is simple and smoothly styled. People move in, they are allowed to dangle things out and change the facade. This develops. They express themselves more and more exotically . . . it becomes spooky and decidedly 'Gothic'. One imagines that a committee of tenants meets and starts to control things, and over the next stages of the cycle the Gothic becomes stylised and then cleaned up. In the end, inevitably, we have returned to something pretty similar to the original tower.

Architecture itself goes round and round – at least in terms of its discussion. The history of interests, the history of responses – to Classicism, to Rationalism, to Functionalism, to Romanticism . . . and you think of the metamorphosis that has occurred within Europe in the last year (in political and social terms) – this cyclic action is both frightening and fascinating.

Arcadia: trickling towers;
Metamorphosis, 1978

18

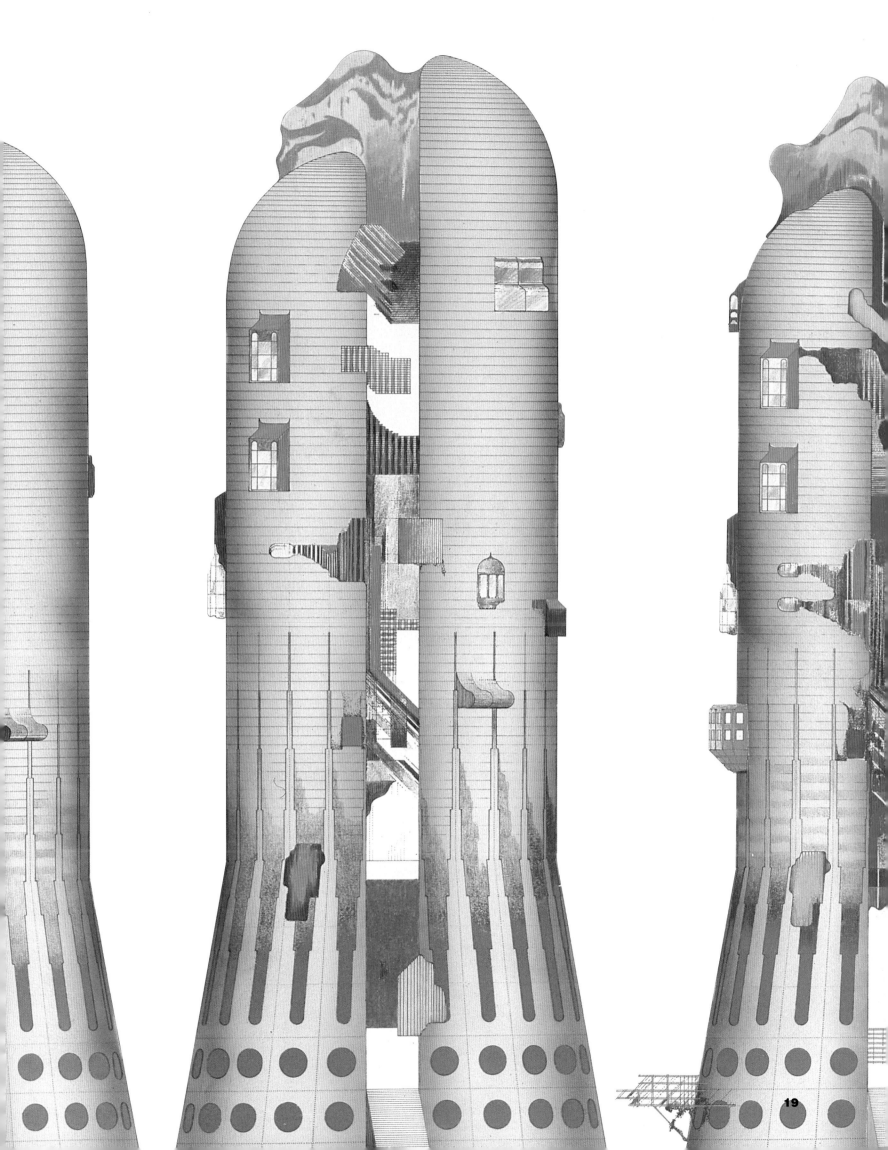

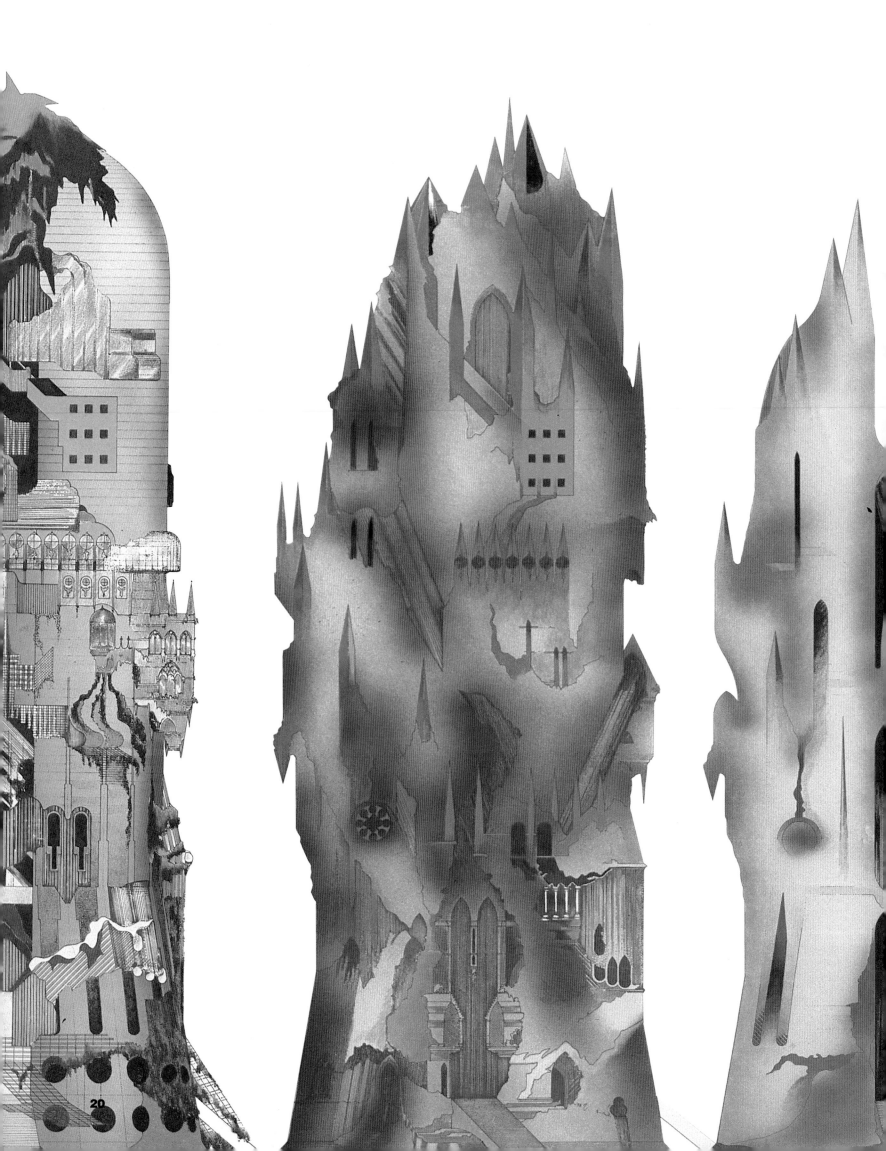

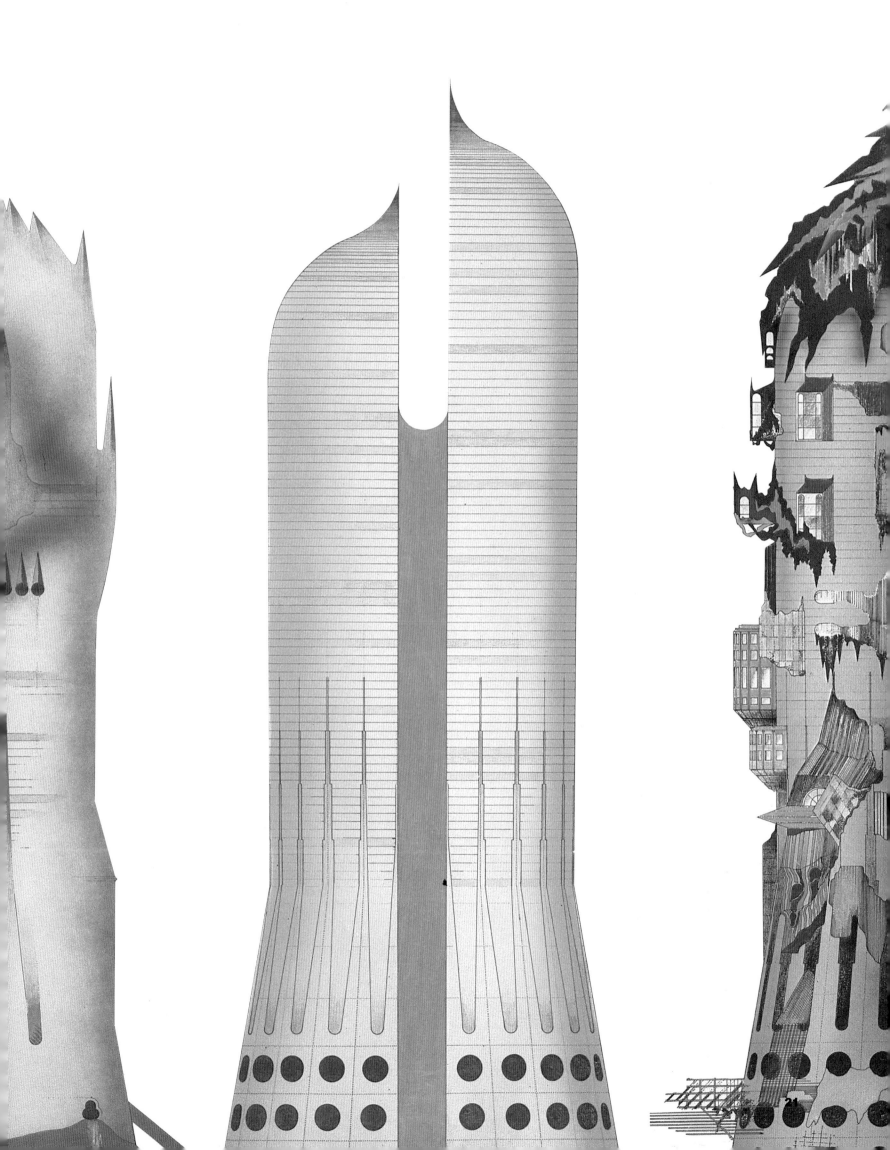

So it was that I designed, very early in my career, a thing called 'Plug-in City'. You plug it in and pull it out. Bits of it come and go, so it can be said to involve metamorphosis, though the basic structure is on a long-stay cycle and the capsules on a short-stay cycle. Looking at it more than 20 years on, I still find much of the proposition is OK. The action is a little too 'jerky' for my present taste, and the marshland is a more subtle model, but I must admit that the gentle metamorphic process would be very hard to manage architecturally, whereas the 'Plug-in City' is essentially *hierarchical* and rather ordered and rather consistent, despite its involvement with the idea of 'change'. The child of Buckminster Fuller and Louis Kahn. Indeed, there's much of Kahn in it, certainly of his Philadelphia project (with the triangulated structuring) and of the Medical Center. Eight years later, I re-examined the proposition of the structured armature filled with prefabricated and changeable elements, and made a series of staged drawings (as with 'Addhox' and the tower). In this case, I mentally encouraged the *total* metamorphosis of the thing . . . from nice, neat, constructed elements towards the random, the tatty, the loose, the vegetated (which I shall come on to later), and eventually a state of such laxity and meltedness that in the end it resembles a moon landscape more than anything else. In terms of the storyline, one then asks 'Is the last stage the total end of the civilisation suggested by the first stage? Or is it a much more subtle formation of the architecture?'

   To see what happens as something metamorphoses, as it disintegrates, as it softens, as it grows, as pieces start to hang off or to come away – this examination continues through to recent work.

Plug-in City, 1964

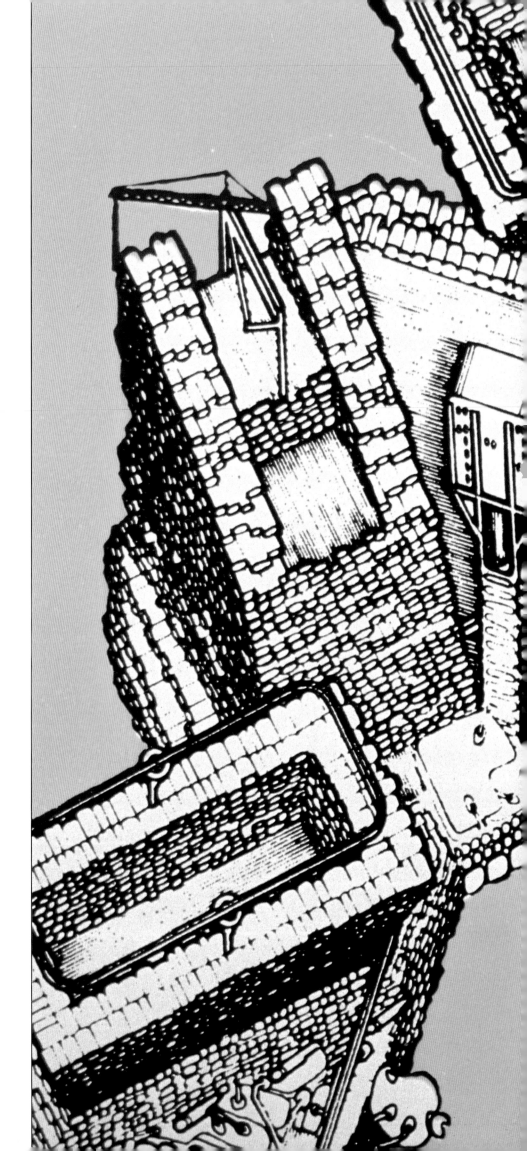

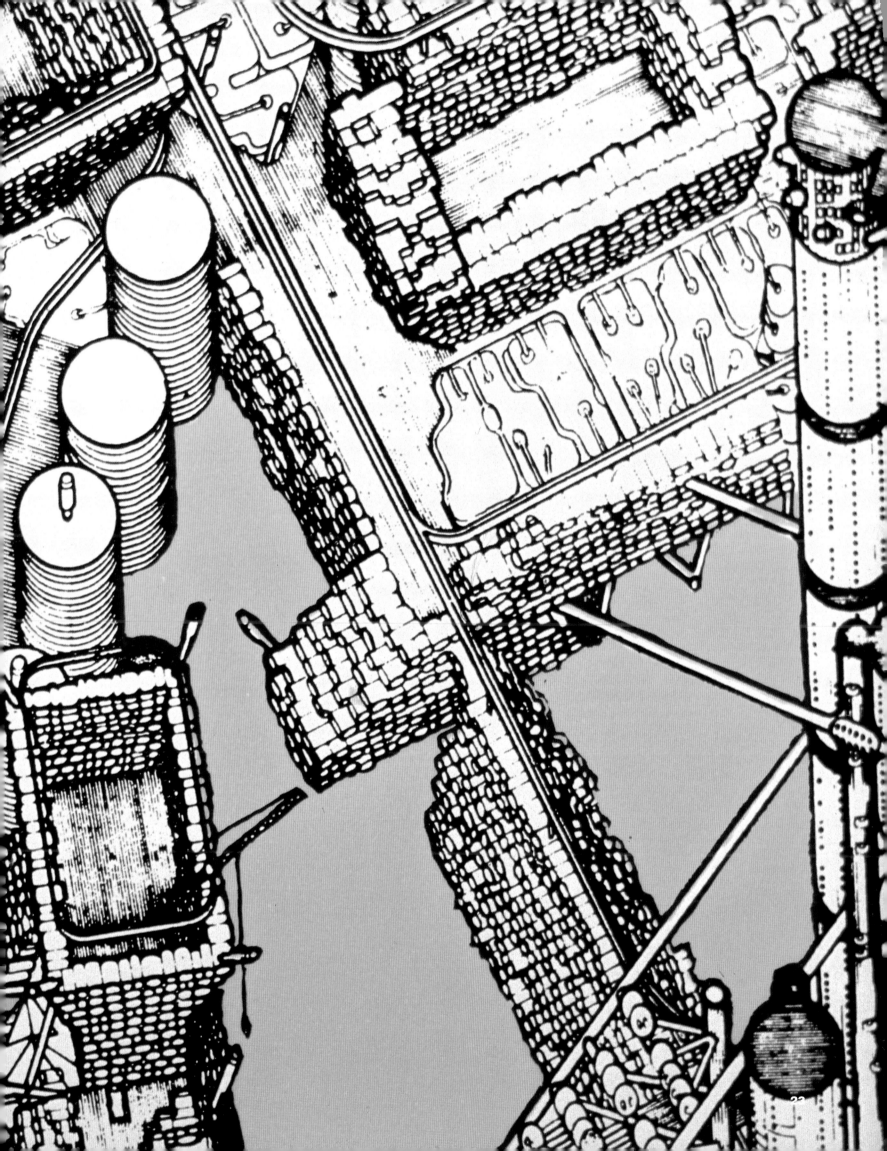

It was applied in 1988 to a piece of what was (until recently) West Berlin. In fact a very *western* part of West Berlin. A funny part, forgotten railway territory behind a small lake which is surrounded by bourgeois villas. We have a word that describes it perfectly: 'brooding'. Somewhere where you can only brood in dark contemplation. My attack upon this place was to say 'Let's take this Western place at the west end of the Kurfürstendamm, propped-up for so many years by the West . . . and let's Westernise it . . . take a piece of America to it. Let's give it a grid, a skyscraper and a square.'

But then, something else as well. A counteractive force, with its own physiology and motives. This item is derived from another aspect of the West – the CACTUS. It is generated from two node points: one is the small island in the lake, the other is the centrifugal point of the autobahn crossing. These very different systems, the orthogonal and the creeping, need each other in order, perhaps, to create an architecture that is really responsive. So as the cycle of the project develops, the American grid and its 'corporate architecture' origins, hang on . . . but the cactus architecture does increasingly strange things to it. In the Plug-in City there is a far closer family relationship between the parts. Here, the counteractive forces engage in some kind of counterpoint . . . the straight and the insidious . . . creeping, virus-like. Hybrids develop.

The fungoid growth is also the child of my architectural method: toy . . . animal. I like the cactus. I like the idea of cactus as architecture. Marvellous! The Cactus. Nasty, spiky, funny, blobby – the only architects who've really done anything close to cactus architecture are probably the Brazilians.

Way Out West, Berlin, 1988

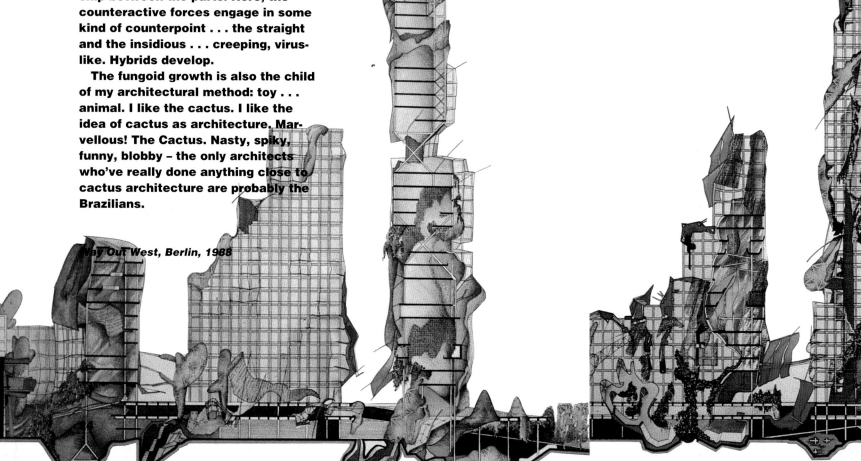

25

Looking at the thing in detail, we find the old railway lines still there, overlaid by the deck and the shafts and drapes of the new buildings. As they metamorphose, the cactus not only intervenes, but in the process becomes itself, transmogrified, becomes more stretched and useful. The skyscraper itself absorbs the cactus architecture and begins to absorb the vegetation as well. Frames and rooms and skins are the product. There is still some order left. We are playing with the issues of flexing, collage skinning . . . all in the process of change, of course.

The ground plan also starts to transfer itself onto the vertical plane. From time to time there are still quite ordinary pieces of building. The metamorphosis occurs according to the concept of the West. The America of the early eastern mould is replaced by that of Arizona; the *real* West. So the inevitable title of the project is 'Way Out West – Berlin'. East Coast culture is preoccupied with Europe anyway. It so happens that I am rather scared in the desert, myself. Just as I am rather scared by heights. So the design of such a thing is a certain sustainable nightmare as well as indulgence! Design is, when it is going really well, a nervous business.

29

CONVERSATION 3
VEGETATION AND LANDSCAPE

Pleasure Gardens, Bournemouth

My next preoccupation runs around the issue of vegetation and landscape, but I should amplify the definition: I mean vegetation *as an architectural artefact* and landscape as *urbanism*. Speaking often, in far-flung places, I have to state that my own fascination with vegetation and landscape is a love of that vegetation and landscape with which I am comfortable, and familiar, so that I can do *uncomfortable* things with it. So I can normally deal best with a landscape which is soft, gentle, damp – the unextreme landscape of Northern Europe. This can then be pushed to very strange conditions. I suspect that building in the desert or on a mountain, I would be very orthodox, seeking comfort in the ordinary.

Choosing the illustrations for this sort of conversation, I found one where I felt tremendously nostalgic and comfortable; a little stream running between areas of well-prepared grass, well dampened, and random trees, not exotic, not famous, but very calming.

It is part of one's own culture, the ambiguity of soft and mysterious views, which the painter Turner understood better than I. In a garden view, seen in the mist, the foreground contains some topiary: bushes ordered by man – certainly not as God grew them. The middle ground contains neat, identifiable trees. Well-disciplined but not subject to hairdressing. In the further distance are quite wild trees. And what lurks within them? Man, animal, monster, architecture? The Turneresque issue is of degrees of freedom, of wildness, of mystery, of definition . . . of not *quite* knowing. Rather like the elliptical conversation and the elliptical criticism, the possibilities exist out there – continuously open-ended and liable to gain sustenance from sources so disparate as to be only limited by the imagination. Then one returns, gradually to the foreground and towards the territory of control and definition.

Germane to this admixture of taste and speculation is a direct pairing of images from England on the one hand and Japan on the other. I love Japan, and the more I go there the more I find tremendous parallels between the two: they are both wet and crowded islands, for instance; they both have long and consistent cultures; they both have a love-hate relationship with the mainland from which so much – but not all – of their cultures derive.

It is a heady experience to feel the pervasive refinement – even mannerism – of Japan. I can extrapolate from the fact that the English have chosen to get the European rhetoric wrong, deliberately choosing to be less polemical, deliberately choosing to distort the broad sweeps of philosophical and political movements, deliberately standing them up and then folding them back into themselves – like the landscape.

But after all, in both places the landscape and the garden are not as God made them: there are 2,000 (maybe 4,000) years of battles, of sick cows, of the third son of the second son who was maybe stupid (and did stupid things to his field), and the clever man (who did clever things with his field). The group of monks who invented the myth of a secret in order to get money. Somebody who planted hedges. So who knows how many layers of chance and circumstance, or weather and husbandry lie in a picture of English (or Japanese) landscape?

English Garden

Japanese Garden

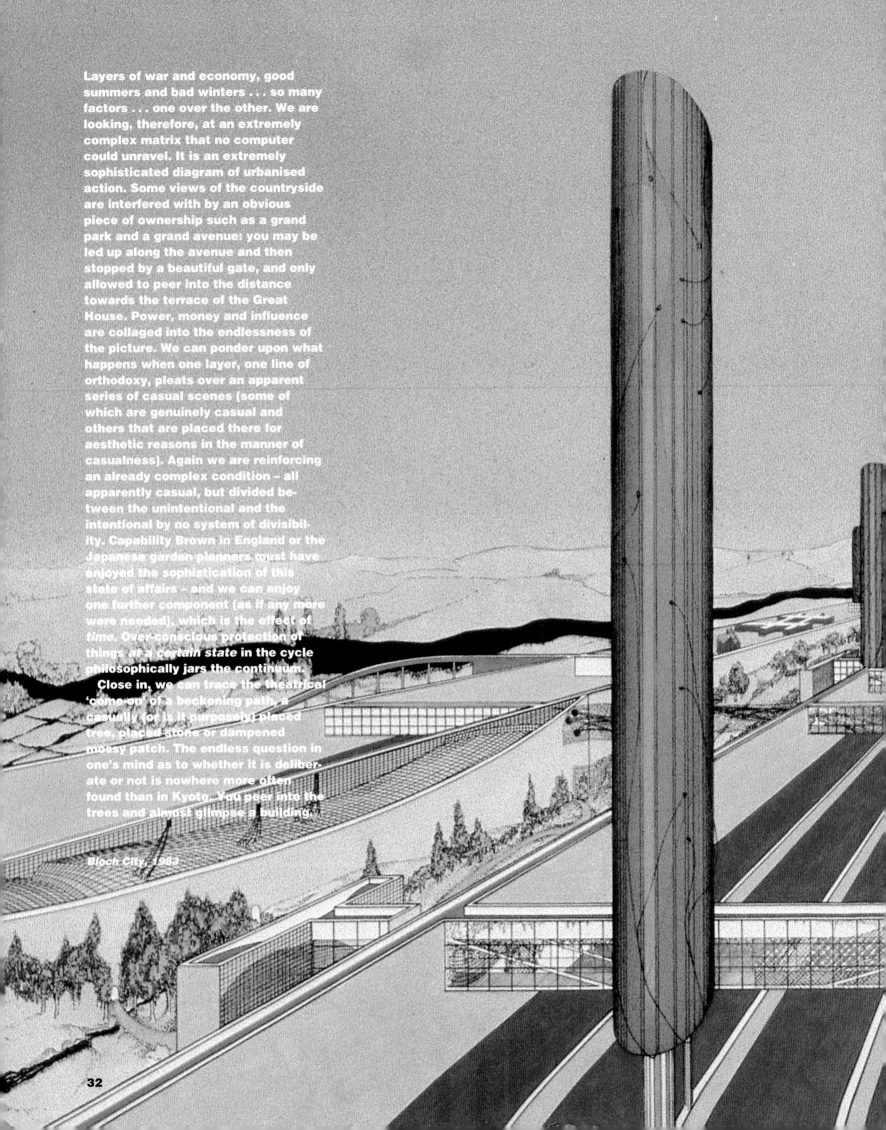

Layers of war and economy, good summers and bad winters . . . so many factors . . . one over the other. We are looking, therefore, at an extremely complex matrix that no computer could unravel. It is an extremely sophisticated diagram of urbanised action. Some views of the countryside are interfered with by an obvious piece of ownership such as a grand park and a grand avenue: you may be led up along the avenue and then stopped by a beautiful gate, and only allowed to peer into the distance towards the terrace of the Great House. Power, money and influence are collaged into the endlessness of the picture. We can ponder upon what happens when one layer, one line of orthodoxy, pleats over an apparent series of casual scenes (some of which are genuinely casual and others that are placed there for aesthetic reasons in the manner of casualness). Again we are reinforcing an already complex condition – all apparently casual, but divided between the unintentional and the intentional by no system of divisibility. Capability Brown in England or the Japanese garden planners must have enjoyed the sophistication of this state of affairs – and we can enjoy one further component (as if any more were needed), which is the effect of *time*. Over-conscious protection of things *at a certain state* in the cycle philosophically jars the continuum.

Close in, we can trace the theatrical 'come-on' of a beckoning path, a casually (or is it purposely) placed tree, placed stone or dampened mossy patch. The endless question in one's mind as to whether it is deliberate or not is nowhere more often found than in Kyoto. You peer into the trees and almost glimpse a building.

Bloch City, 1983

32

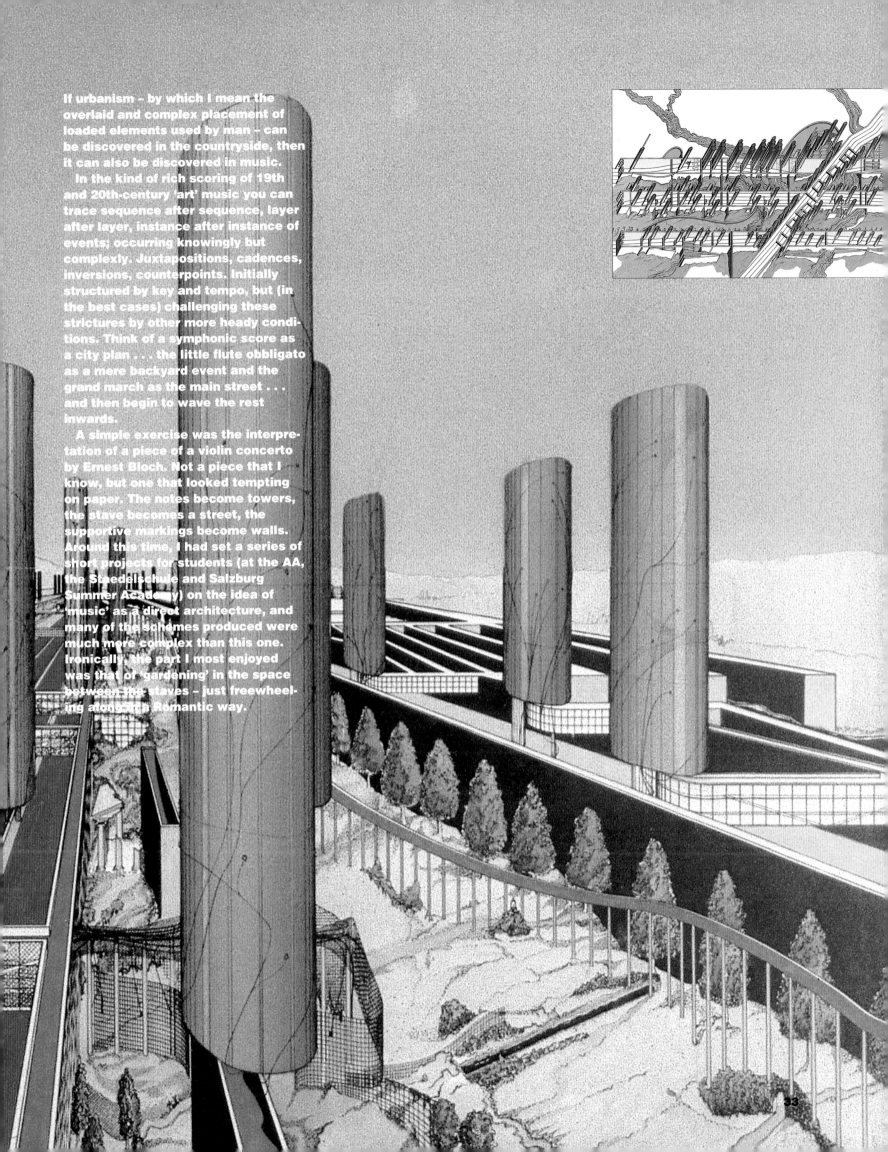

If urbanism – by which I mean the overlaid and complex placement of loaded elements used by man – can be discovered in the countryside, then it can also be discovered in music.

In the kind of rich scoring of 19th and 20th-century 'art' music you can trace sequence after sequence, layer after layer, instance after instance of events; occurring knowingly but complexly. Juxtapositions, cadences, inversions, counterpoints. Initially structured by key and tempo, but (in the best cases) challenging these strictures by other more heady conditions. Think of a symphonic score as a city plan . . . the little flute obbligato as a mere backyard event and the grand march as the main street . . . and then begin to wave the rest inwards.

A simple exercise was the interpretation of a piece of a violin concerto by Ernest Bloch. Not a piece that I know, but one that looked tempting on paper. The notes become towers, the stave becomes a street, the supportive markings become walls. Around this time, I had set a series of short projects for students (at the AA, the Staedelschule and Salzburg Summer Academy) on the idea of 'music' as a direct architecture, and many of the schemes produced were much more complex than this one. Ironically, the part I most enjoyed was that of 'gardening' in the space between the staves – just freewheeling along in a Romantic way.

So to 'layering'. Sometimes layers occur in the placement of objects in a conscious 'foreground' or 'middleground'. Sometimes there is the sense of distance rather than position. The view begging the presence (or even existence) of a plan.

In the project, Layer City, one set up a series of formal sequences and informal cadences. A wide variety of matrices – grids, terracing, axes, swathes, series, broken series – were scrambled or deliberately made to collide. There are, of course, vestiges of the 19th-century urban method involving the street and the strip of path; the boulevard and the planted monument; watercourses falling down steep terrain (I placed the Layer City somewhere along the Oslo Fjord); meshing and folding. The road system took the form of a musical bar structure that became focused only at the seaward tip of the city and there, perversely perhaps, the downtown stands fragmented, its feet in the sea.

The business of layering can be thought of as a technique or a process: a type of knitting with the three-dimensional as well as the dynamic collage in mind.

In the project for a 'museum in a garden in the sky', which I started for a site on the Westhaven in Frankfurt and then reinterpreted for the competition for Kawasaki (near Tokyo), the layering process was central to every aspect of the thing. Vegetation became a mere necessity.

We can look at Castle Drogo in Devon. The gardens of this Lutyens building prepare – using trimmed hedges – a series of stage-like zones; as carefully prepared and tailored as anything produced in steel, wood or stone. At the end, there is a chink through which one sees the rolling Devon countryside: a mixture of control and endlessness.

By contrast, we can pursue the possibility of the architectural element as an *insertion* into the landscape, existing, perhaps, in a crevice and therefore challenging the tradition of the building as a focal point in the landscape.

Shadow House (Cook & Hawley)

Shadow House (Cook & Hawley)

Shadow House, drawing by Christine Hawley

Background: Shadow House, drawing by Christine Hawley

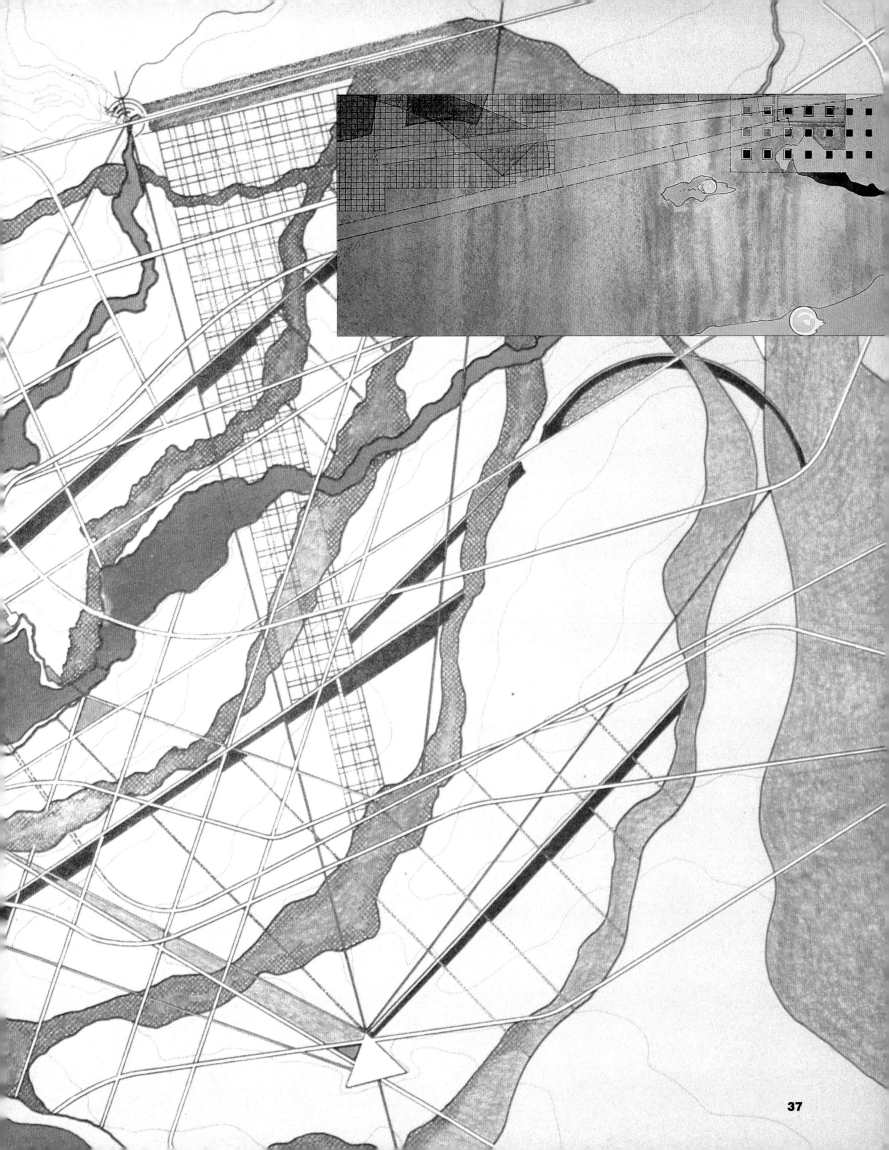

37

It can be quite a highly organised
building, if we wish. In the 'Urban
Mark' project, there were vegetable
buildings in tandem with 'normal'
buildings. In the 'Prepared Landscape'
there is a complex building resting
inside the landscape, with strands of
vegetation dropping down amongst it.

Prepared Landscape

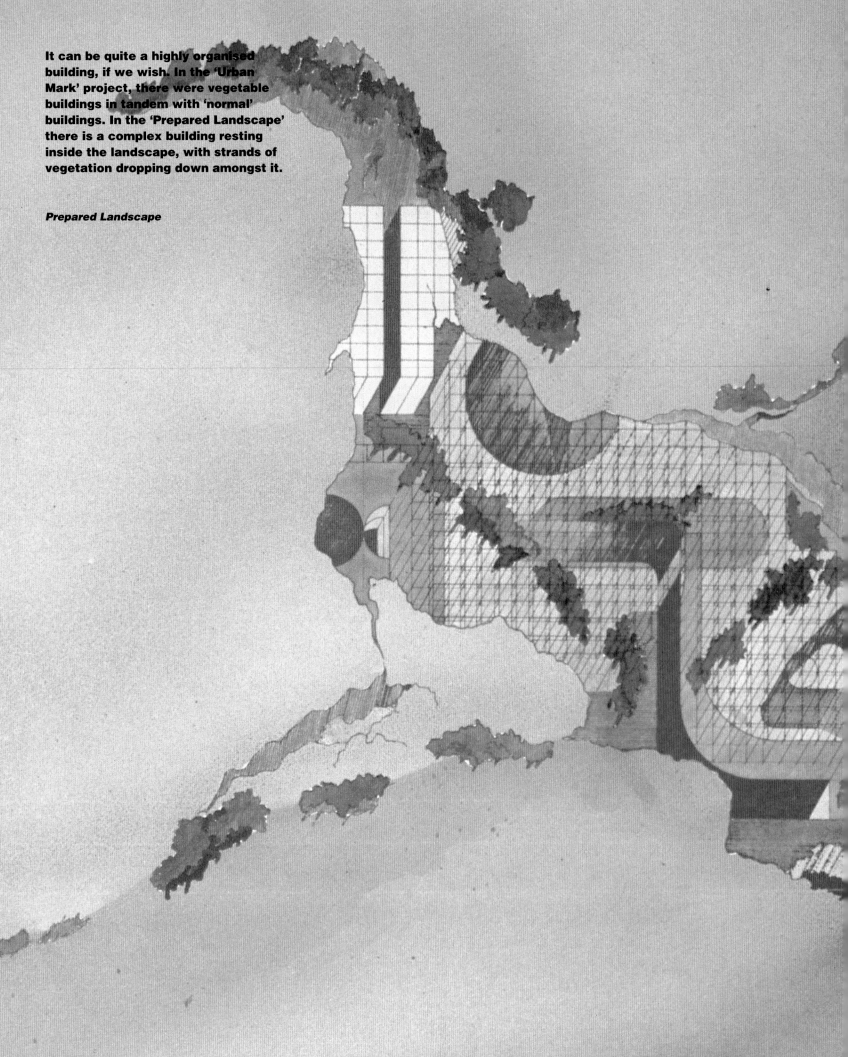

Urban Mark, 1972

Approaching from another direction, however, I sought out a condition that seemed to have no history, no loading: 'the LUMP'. Remember that the mere 'lump' has none of the dynamics of a 'heap' nor the deliberateness of a 'pile'. It's just a nothing – no physiognomy – just a lump! After I had made the project, a drawing was found by the English artist Hurst Walker entitled *I Love the Lump* and when I visited the National Gallery in Oslo I found all sorts of Norwegian painters paying homage to selected lumps in the landscape of the fjords. So one was unwittingly the child of a whole tradition of lump-lovers. In presenting my own lump I take you round from the first face where, if you look hard, you might see the odd insertion of 'constructed' objects . . . to the second face where there are more – and some of them surely skylights . . . to the third face which is the give-away: a path leading to an entrance. The thing was a building all the time! One has gone through a cycle, starting by saying, 'I'm going to take something that is totally abstract and has nothing to do with anything and make it into a building. I am too old and architectural to be totally 'lumpist'; in the end I make another architecture.

From this point on I became interested in the conjunction of lumpy, stuffed 'Slurrrp' architecture with normal architecture. The easiest example – from the breakfast table – is that of scrambled egg on toast. What's nice about it is that it is so imperfect. The scrambled egg soaks into part of the toast and lies awkwardly over another part. In this particular case the egg is the 'lump' architecture and the toast is a regular strip of office building. The result becomes a model for later conjunctions such as 'Way Out West – Berlin' and the Breitscheidplatz project for the same city.

Lump sequence, office block

From all of this came 'Sponge' (son of 'Lump'). In this slightly more complex project the initial idea was to take existing buildings and strip off the outer skin and then to reintroduce a spongey, landscape-like zone with a variety of skins. This led, inevitably, to a completely new building type – not needing the pre-existent framework – where the more 'floppy' architecture is interdependent with its own core of more stable architecture. Various analogies and sub-types suggest themselves, such as the 'patchwork' (as in patchwork quilt: made up of standard sized panels but widely different derivations); 'gunge' (already discussed) and the first version of the 'sleek corner' (a deliberate exercise in the aesthetics of artificiality finding an analogy between an architectural skin and the cosmeticised face of the 18th-century coquette or Japanese Kabuki actor). The term 'sponge' is derived from that which you find in the bath (with the capability to absorb). It is another device to encourage the ambiguous condition.

Sponge Steps

The nearest that the Archigram Group
came to making a large building was
in winning the competition for the
Monte Carlo Entertainments Centre.
Aborted after nearly three years'
work, it would not have put our imagery on the face of the Mediterranean coast, for it was to be completely buried underground. The aim
was to maintain the landscape of this
piece of precious, reclaimed land. The
secret building would be inside with
its robots and other apparatus at the
disposal of the show producer to
create the architecture-of-the-mo-
ment. Over time, certain bits and
pieces began to creep out of the
ground as we worked on it, but in
retrospect it was the purest version
with the total 'black box' that was the
strongest. A key idea was also that of
riddling the ground with a series of
'golf-holes' – in effect multi-channel
plugs for a special closed-circuit
viewing-listening device, the show
inside the ground becoming available
(selectively) above the ground. From
this time onwards the interaction of
not only architecture-with-landscape
but devices-with-architecture-with-
landscape was established in one's
mind. One's mind remains somewhat
ambiguously directed, of course. Half
of me wishes the thing to be complete
and totally hidden – the other half
enjoys inconsistency and the trailing
of clues.

*Roosevelt Island Housing, New York City,
1975 (Project by Peter Cook, Ron Herron,
Christine Hawley, Ingrid Morris, Tom
Heneghan, Penny Richards, John Robins,
Gerry Whale, Keith Priest). Aerial view
drawn by Gerry Whale.*

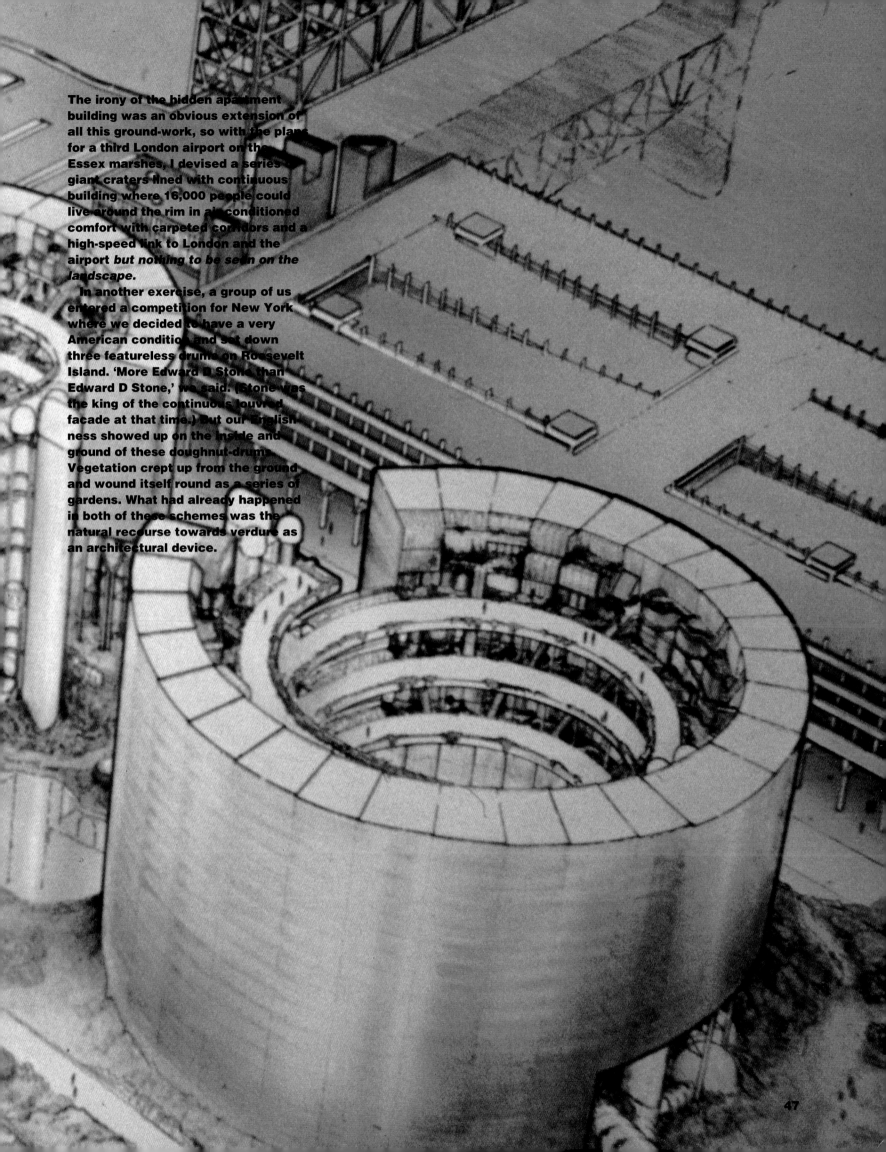

The irony of the hidden apartment building was an obvious extension of all this ground-work, so with the plans for a third London airport on the Essex marshes, I devised a series of giant craters lined with continuous building where 16,000 people could live around the rim in air-conditioned comfort with carpeted corridors and a high-speed link to London and the airport *but nothing to be seen on the landscape.*

In another exercise, a group of us entered a competition for New York where we decided to have a very American condition and set down three featureless drums on Roosevelt Island. 'More Edward D Stone than Edward D Stone,' we said. (Stone was the king of the continuous 'louvred' facade at that time.) But our English-ness showed up on the inside and ground of these doughnut-drums. Vegetation crept up from the ground and wound itself round as a series of gardens. What had already happened in both of these schemes was the natural recourse towards verdure as an architectural device.

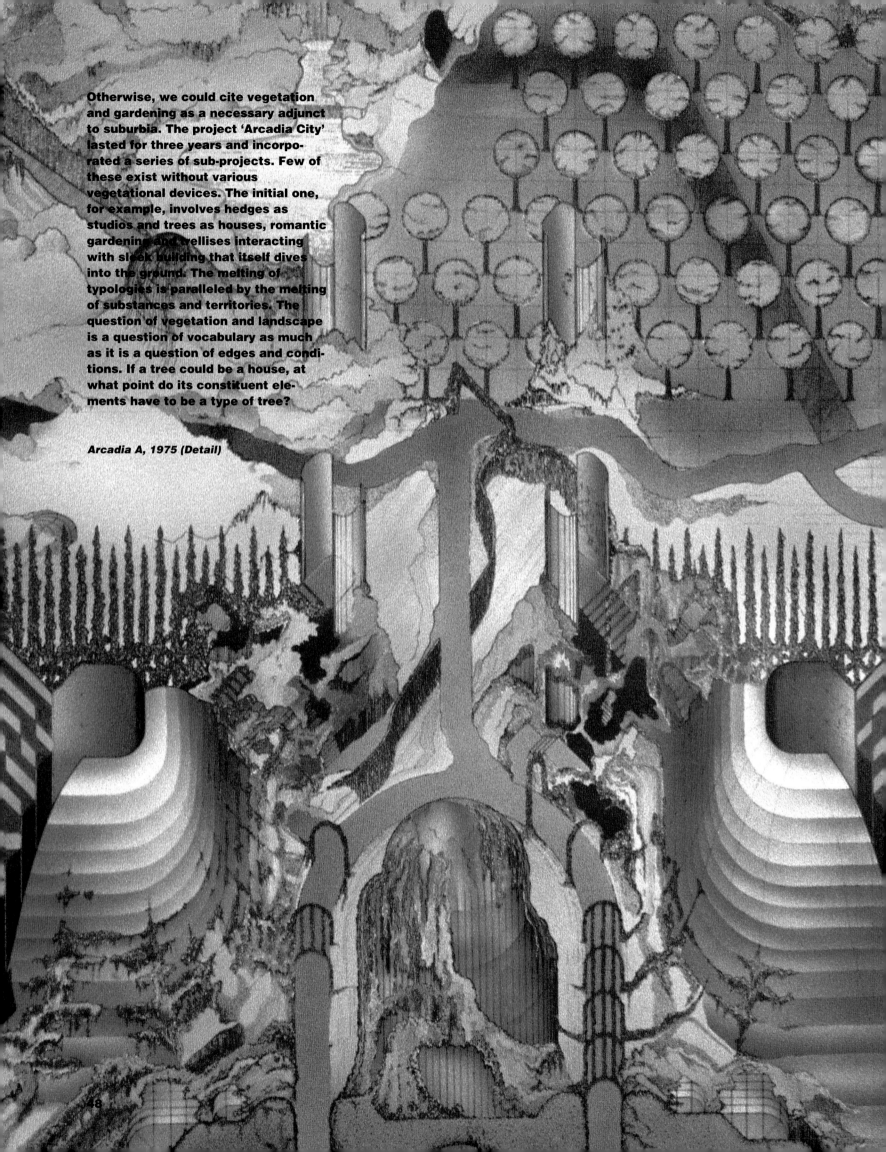

Otherwise, we could cite vegetation and gardening as a necessary adjunct to suburbia. The project 'Arcadia City' lasted for three years and incorporated a series of sub-projects. Few of these exist without various vegetational devices. The initial one, for example, involves hedges as studios and trees as houses, romantic gardening and trellises interacting with sleek building that itself dives into the ground. The melting of typologies is paralleled by the melting of substances and territories. The question of vegetation and landscape is a question of vocabulary as much as it is a question of edges and conditions. If a tree could be a house, at what point do its constituent elements have to be a type of tree?

Arcadia A, 1975 (Detail)

48

49

I am fascinated by the Gardens at Schwezingen (near Mannheim) and the orangery in the grounds of the Castle of Karlsruhe. In these gardens there are trellises that take on vegetation and then frame up to an avenue that is terminated by a 'trompe l'oeil' picture painted onto a wall and discreetly lit. Neoclassicism, fakery and seasonal growth all occur together. At Karlsruhe the long wall which contains a restaurant, is approached by a large ironwork structure, like the framework for a glazed building. But there seems to be (deliberately) no glazing and instead the framework is laced with branches that in summer create a vegetated room. It is not unlike the Via Appia house that was the first collaborative project of the Cook and Hawley office.

The idea of the street frontage being well hedged, so that no one knows what is going on behind it, is an English theme. In the 'House of Two Studios' I hid all sorts of things in the back of the hedge creating a secret world behind the hedge that was effectively a theatre set, viewed from the house. Part of the hedge actually became a usable room. In this sense it was a double or treble

House of Two Studios 1981

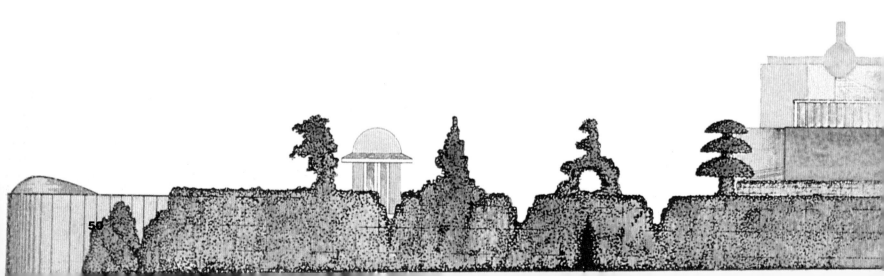

play: apparently relaxed architecture reinforcing a much more classical layout than I would normally make, the garden being a complete part of the architectural composition and the public 'hints' of the building being particularly selective. A few months later I took a group of students to Los Angeles and, dutifully, we went to photograph the Greene and Greene houses at Pasadena. My excitement lay across the street from one of the houses: here was a hedge-house intact and intriguing. 'Is there really a house in that hedge?' You may ask such a question, but I deliberately won't give you an answer: for my purposes, the formation and scale of the hedge in question is sufficient to support the idea. As to the scant attention to Greene and Greene on my part (35 cameras were pointing away from the hedge), you take yourself with you: architectural travelling is both a process of introduction and verification.

Parallels between the degree of formality (or heroism) of a building and the soft disintegration that can be moulded out of ground and bushes, trees, rocks or terraces are by now essential to the designing system.

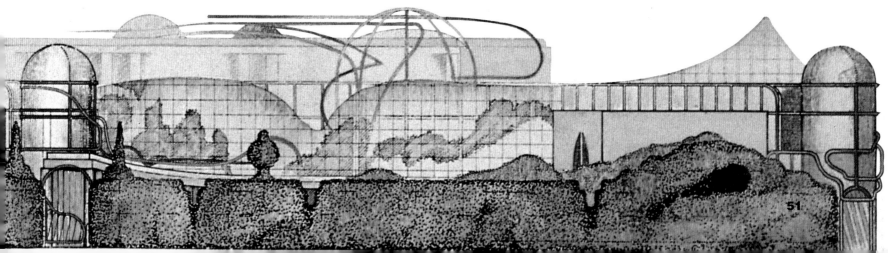

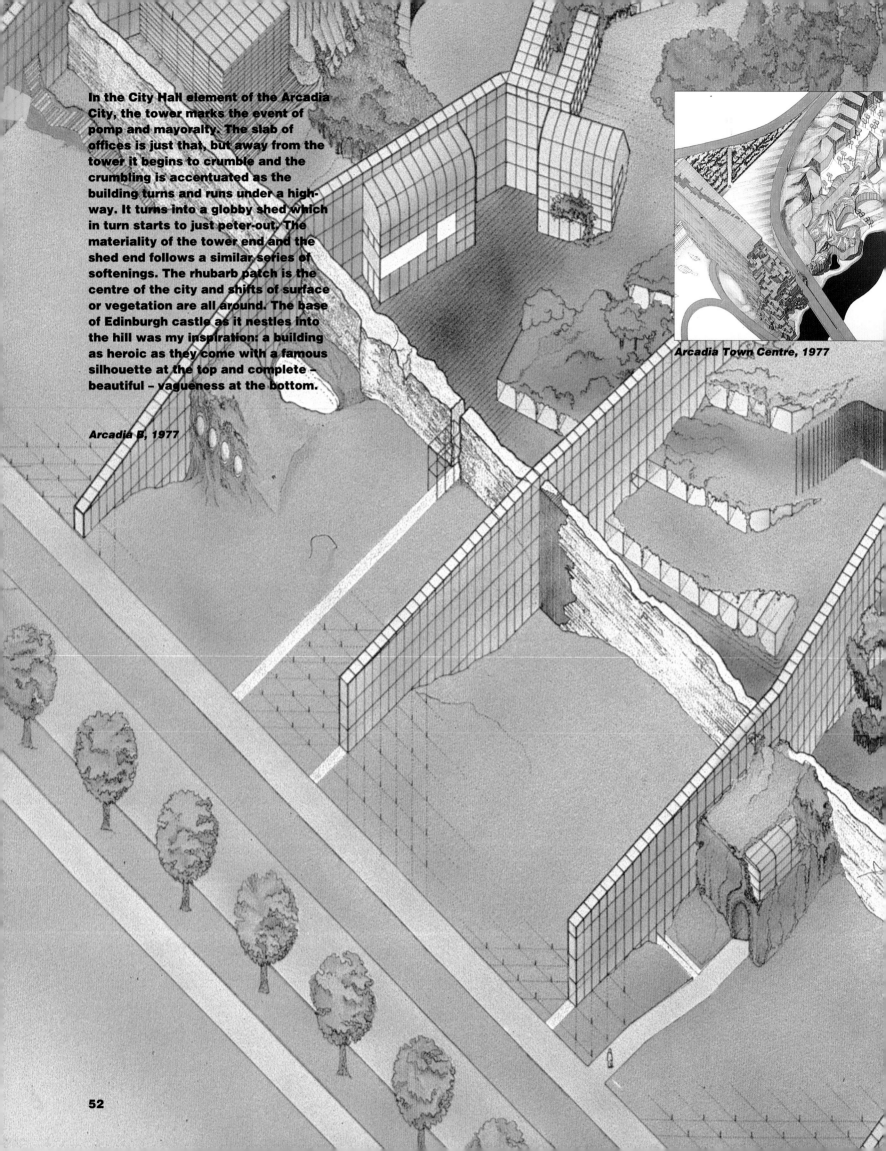

In the City Hall element of the Arcadia City, the tower marks the event of pomp and mayoralty. The slab of offices is just that, but away from the tower it begins to crumble and the crumbling is accentuated as the building turns and runs under a highway. It turns into a globby shed which in turn starts to just peter-out. The materiality of the tower end and the shed end follows a similar series of softenings. The rhubarb patch is the centre of the city and shifts of surface or vegetation are all around. The base of Edinburgh castle as it nestles into the hill was my inspiration: a building as heroic as they come with a famous silhouette at the top and complete – beautiful – vagueness at the bottom.

Arcadia B, 1977

Arcadia Town Centre, 1977

52

The Frankfurt-Kawasaki structure, the 'Museum in a Garden in the Sky' returns to the megastructure. We have to remember some dates here. The original Plug-in City originates in a project that David Greene and I made for 'Nottingham Shopping' in 1962. This is the first moment that we use a crane-railway and shop elements hanging off the 'viaduct'. The 'official' Plug-in City was published in 1964 and certain developments of it continued until late 1966. The first time that I could graphically return to a megastructure was in the 'Urban Mark' – which, as we have already seen, was a form of critique or apocryphal tale. The Museum in the Sky was designed in 1986 . . . a clear 20 years since Plug-in. Am I being slow? Does one need 20 years to fall back in love with an idea? Or is it as much a question of labels? Or boredom? Whatever the reason, I had no hesitation in suggesting a giant steel structure which could be served by lifts and escalators rising out of an industrial or downtown city landscape. In both the German and Japanese sites there was a dockside location and flat land around, with undistinguished buildings in the immediate vicinity. In many ways it was also a *cri de coeur* for some fresh thinking about muse-

Real City, Frankfurt, Skyglade, Westhafen, 1986 (Reworked as Kawasaki Information Museum)

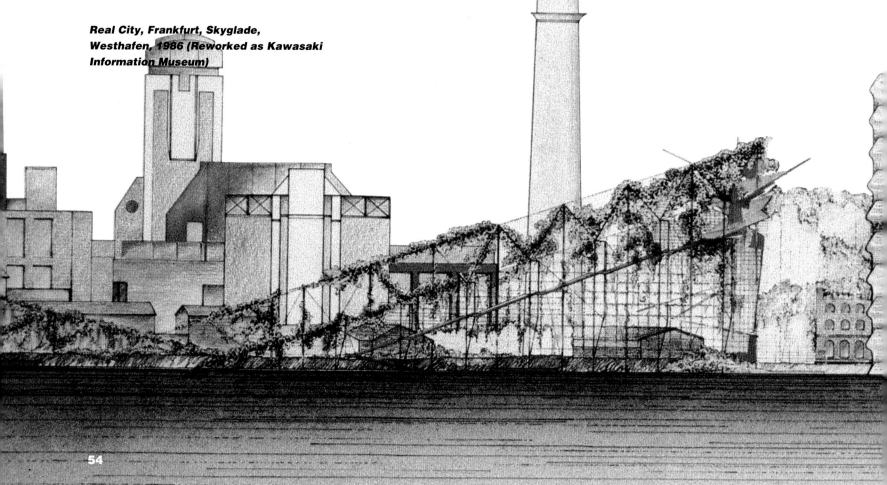

ums, surrounded as I was by the very tight interpretations being encouraged in Frankfurt. Why not have a museum like a park, or the Japanese garden, where you proceed in a very relaxed way from discrete item to discrete item, or even choose to dally in between. It was also another essay in the alternatives to full frontality. Armatures run across the dock as well, with galleries that contain a random mixture of windows with 'real' views and simulated 'windows' with invented views, deliberately confusing reality with myth. The built objects and the greenery are woven together (as in Karlsruhe), the building and structure mesh together – the spaces are more often created by the vegetation mass than by anything else. The little triangulated and brightly-coloured pavilions are then back in the role of the tiny constructed elements on the Lump: architecture as an incidental part of the total structure. So what of the potentials and limits of a megastructure now? At last, it is taking on a more subtle role, enabling us to break out from the tyranny of the ground plane, enabling us to create a magical experience in space, enabling the *unlike* to sit with the *unlike*.

FORMAL SHOW-HOUSES

HIGHLY CONTROLLABLE SPACES FOR SPECIAL EVENTS

SELECTED ELEMENT

FINGER-WALKS

REAL VIEW= WINDOW

AMONGST SERIES OF PROGRAMMED IMAGES

DRAPES OF SPACE
DRAPES OF GARDEN
DRAPES OF INFORMA

S.E

Kawasaki Information Museum

KAWASAKI ADVANCED INFORMATION CITY : INTELLIGENT PLA

ART GALLERIES	6	SWIMMING / SAILING	7	ATMOSPHERICALLY CONTRIVED 'SET-PIECE'	8	TYPICAL MUSEUM
"serious stuff"		"healthy types"		"culture"		"keeps on.. and o
PARKS / ZOOS	9	DOING NOTHING IN PARTICULAR	10	EATING-DRINKING-SOCIAL GATHERINGS	11	TYPICAL INFORMA
"kids' stuff"		"certainly not serious"		"essential"		still environme

Kawasaki Information Museum

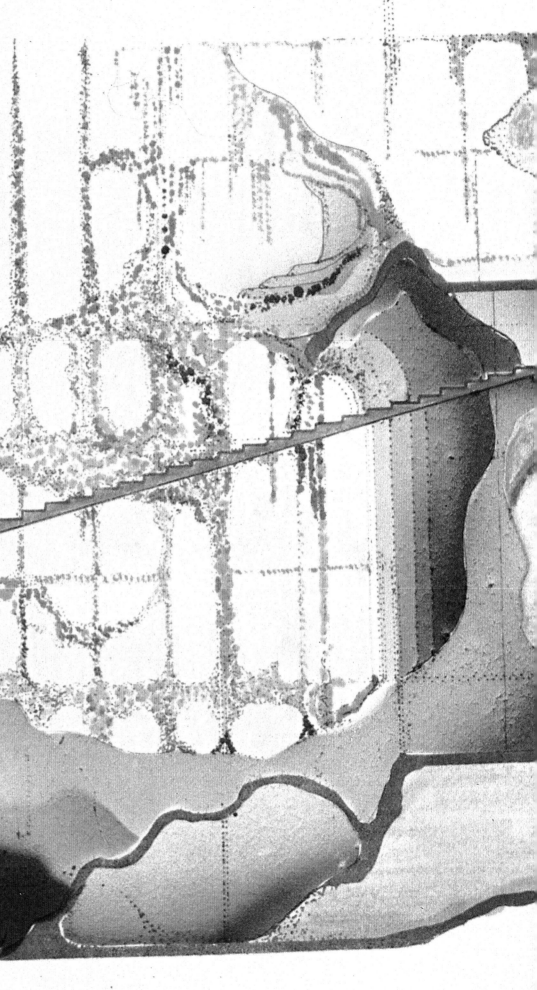

CONVERSATION 4
LAYERS AND
ORCHESTRATIONS

The fascination for layering does not seem to wane over the years. The physical quality of layering, already discussed, allows the possibility of an architectural place that is not just confronted by shapes and blocks and objects and water and things that stop you in your tracks. The phase 'Full Frontal' is its antithesis. In the project designed around 1990 by my partner, Christine Hawley, a sad part of London called Peckham is both site and source of a piece of housing that uses the flotsam and jetsam of a city in decay. Burnt wood, rusting metal, twisted pieces of mechanism and a form of gentle high-tech support come together in a series of layers. Not only is the space layered, but the elements are generically and philosophically layered. Not only this, but you can't tell what is a new piece of building and what is old, what is firm and what is soft.

   So layering is both a spatial issue and also one of attitude; it can take on board both the absurd and less absurd, the soft and nostalgic as well as the shrill and heroic. Plug-in City was concerned with the layering of time, the Museum in the Sky with discovery of the space offered by the sky. The Via Appia House was an exercise in building and garden as one, where the layers were sometimes accentuated (as with the repeated stone chasms on the street side – with their hint of the history of architecture in the form of tiny figures of Roman gods and the modular), and sometimes deliberately melted (as in the 'grotto' area). Perhaps our introduction to the notion, which came through this scheme, was necessarily prompted by a condition of myth and memory. Layering is somehow a 'dreamy' notion. One is tempted therefore to ask the question: are architects put off the idea of a layered architecture by the insistence of many academies upon the idea of order, or are they baffled by the inevitable difficulty of realising an imagined dream in placed, crafted and dimensioned materiality?

Via Appia, 1976 (Cook & Hawley)

ARBOUR

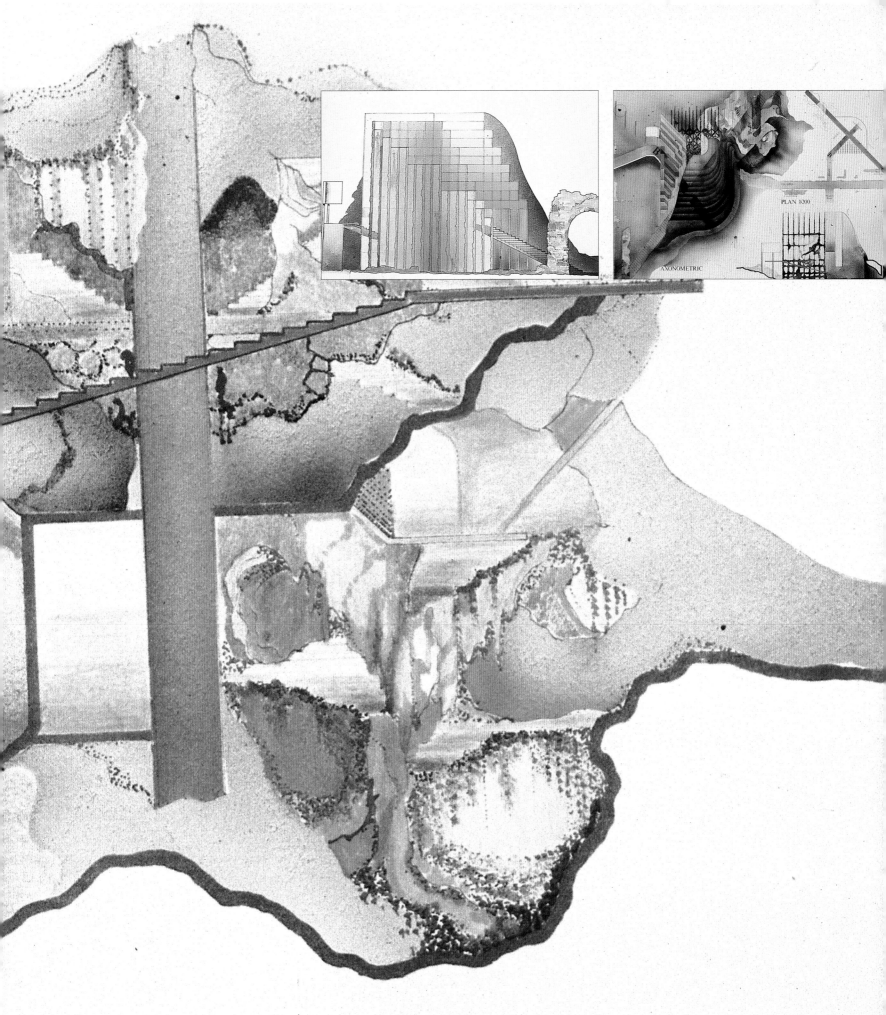

PLAN 1:200

AXONOMETRIC

GROTTO

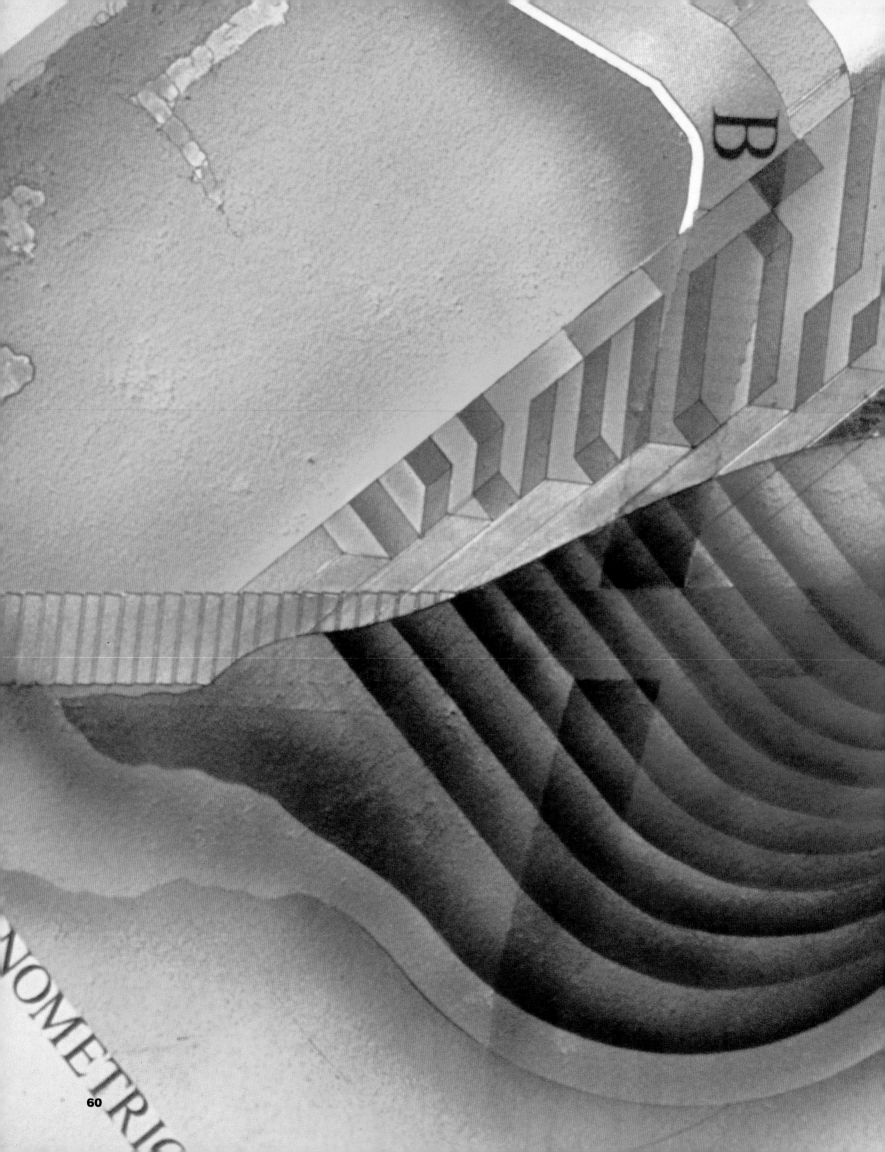

The kinds of sounds that I most enjoy seem to come from the rich scoring of Sibelius or the post-Wagnerian School. In Sibelius, the theme *per se* is often hidden from view (as it were) in the early stages of the Symphony, only to emerge gradually over time. In architectural terms this could mean a building that has little completeness or rhetoric on the facade, but is discoverable and eventually under-standable when you enter within. Indeed, one tends to think of the experience of a building from the starting-point of *being* within it, and some sort of scenario being played-out. Layering is concerned with condition, with time and also with process; you can walk through a building and experience it as theatre.

I took part in an exhibition in Paris, for which many foreign architects were invited to produce projects for that city. I had to use some kind of scenario – for it is a difficult city for the London dweller, inevitably sitting in one's mind as all that London is not; condensed, procedural, elegant, ordered. I erected a constrained place and, with Peter Rice's advice, wrapped a net of glass around five small towers. Each tower revolves – or rather, enables the constituent double-height discs of space to be turned. The apartments within would be tuneable: 'Hey Pierre – let's see the sunset over the Etoile', or, 'My God, I can't stand the sound of the Gouloisiers' dog anymore . . . let's move off 20 degrees'. Within the net is plenty of vegetation, a further devel-opment of hedge houses and the Museum in the Sky. But within *this*, you discover some odd little build-ings. I guess that these are more in

Rotating Housing and Vertical Garden Tower, Paris, 1989

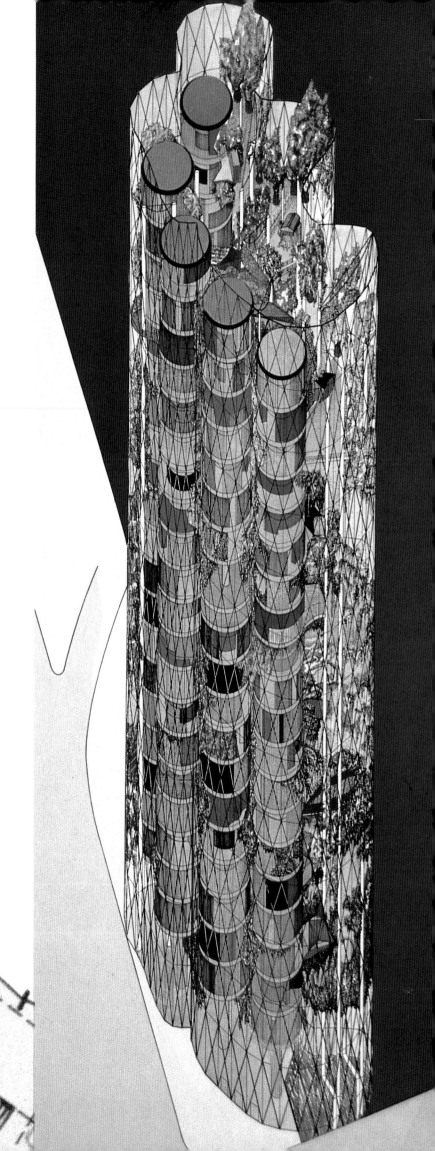

62

the tradition of the English garden shed or the German allotment hut, but the ability to disappear into the outhouse is surely common to many of the bourgeoisie the world over.

So here the layering is on a series of levels: urbanistically, the towers (of which there are still few in Paris) are an insertion into a small crevice of space; architecturally, the stacks of discs are towers within a tower; the garden is a layering of its own – but also a decoy; and the huts the 'home' manqué. From within, the city of Paris is the outer layer beyond the net and beyond the bushes.

The layering process was a continuation of 'Way Out West' – not just a question of metamorphosis, of replacement of object by object; not even of object changing into object, because it is also a process of focusing. The object is focused and defocused, frontality is being covered in layers by veils and the role being played by the parts is in a constant state of change.

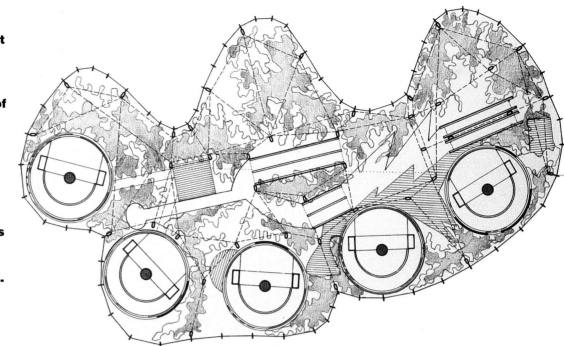

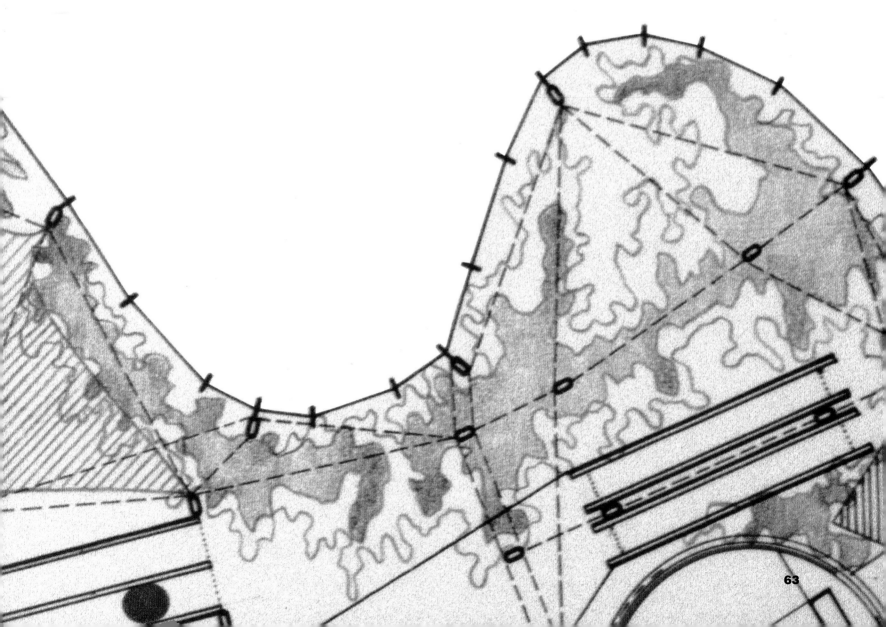

63

CONVERSATION 5
PLACE AND REPARTEE

Repartee is a word deliberately chosen, because we hear plenty about
the idea of 'fitting into' or 'responding
to' the genus loci. But repartee is
altogether a more lively concept.
Repartee implies that you might
(architecturally) give back as good as
you get . . . or better! It might be that
you are (architecturally) aggressive,
or cheeky, or mysterious. But the
building itself must also have a good
old conversation going on with itself.
It must engage in its own repartee of
standpoints and quips and stabs and
parries. Even just going to the toilet in
the middle of the night has a certain
architectural repartee within itself.
Do you want to fumble as you go, or
do you want to have a magical experience . . . as we think you might in our
housing at the Lutzowplatz in Berlin.
   A little town near Frankfurt called
Langen came to Cook and Hawley for
a museum for showing contemporary
stained glass, and based around the
work and contacts of Johannes
Schreiter who lives there. The context is well contrasted: on the north
side the church and a quiet area in
front of the church, the old town hall
and some town houses; on the south
side a ramshackle yard with cars
parked in it and an annual festival
which involves the erection of a large
tent. In a space where there was
demolition to allow for a (now abandoned) road, lies our site. There is no
pokey formal geometry, but the building does not float. Sets of axes
emerge from that of the old town hall,
the street and the yard. There is a
shift between them. The building is

Langen Museum for Stained Glass, 1986
(Cook & Hawley)

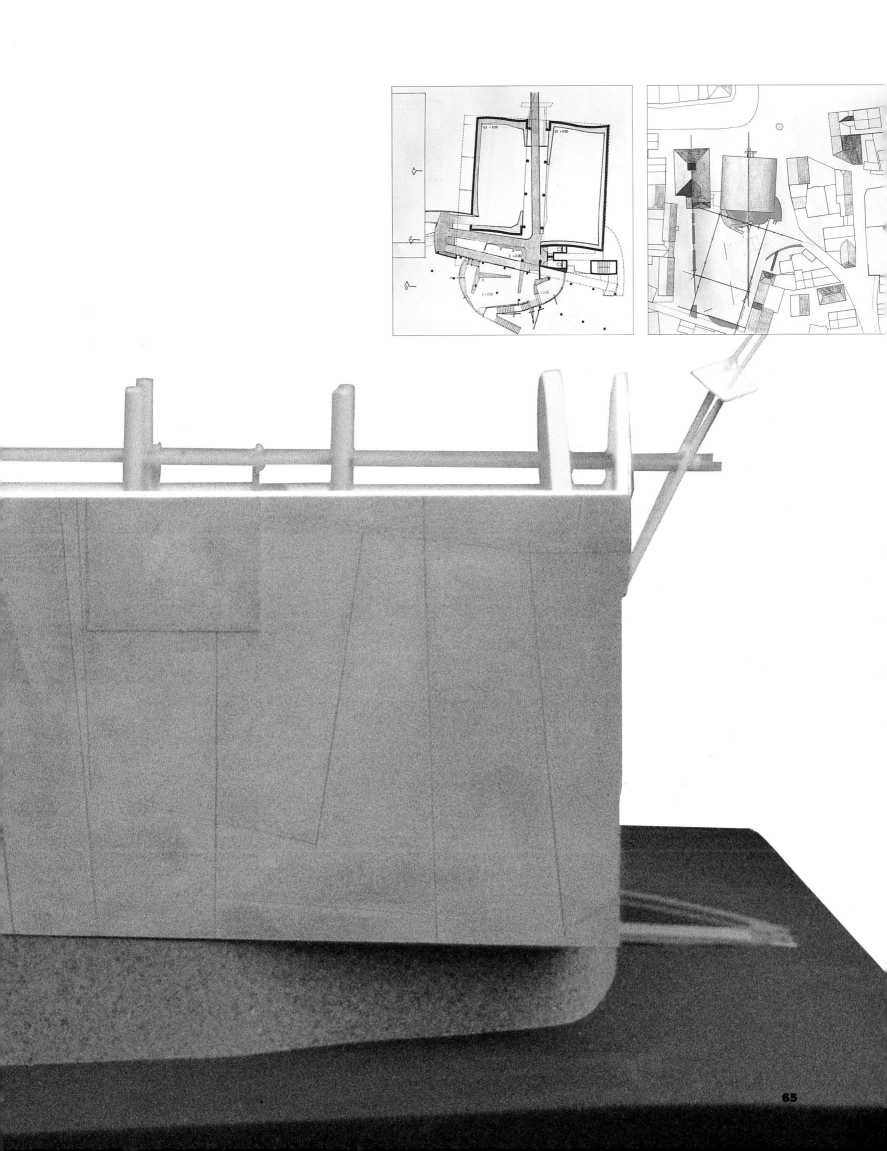

modest, as befits a small town. The artists themselves needed a light-tight box. The town needed a beer cellar (for the older people), a youth club (where the kids could get a drink), a restaurant (where the bour-geoisie could take a glass of wine) and the tent to come once a year, to celebrate the apple-wine festival. So this cultural building is also a set of bars! The walls to the north are as calm as the space they face and a mere chink between them invites you (via the tongue of the glass ramp) to come within. The ramp climbs past the main galleries and then turns, articulating the southern part of the building before climbing further. The south is as voluptuous and carefree in form as the north is restrained. The whole thing is a metal building, a hanging shed, inspired by North American barns . . . indeed it is a form of 'art barn'. The chasm formed to take the entry ramp is also the hoist-ing track, and in the roof are the workshops. During the festival, the tent will be folded over part of the museum and the restaurant will stick out into the tented space – like a tongue. It seems at once a total composition, but tracking the east or west faces the architecture disinte-grates from the tight state to the loose. Its surface, scale and internal discussion were very particular to the business of wandering around brilliant glistening things within the context of a modest place. The rhetoric was that of Jekyll and Hyde: the two charac-ters of the building. This was also true of the Osaka folly (which con-tained other memories of the unbuilt museum), and is also characteristic of our Berlin project.

To build in a square in Berlin is a challenge in itself, but more so when you are surrounded by other architects' new work. Somewhere, through the trees on the other side, is OM Ungers' building; next door are Bangert, Jansen Sholts and Schulz on one flank and Mario Botta on the other; at the rear is Christian de Portzamparc. Within this heavy company, Christine Hawley and I placed ourselves 'within' the scheme and worked from the inside to the outside.

We were told by the IBA Directors that we could extend beyond the building line only with winter gardens. This fascinated us. Both of us could remember working on British local authority housing, squeezing and folding . . . putting prams under stairs, airing cupboards over bulkheads, draining boards over waste chutes. The British are concerned that the person in the kitchen deserves a good view, or even two good views, and we would criticise much of the IBA work as being facade-driven and uncaring about the apartments themselves. The orientation is east-west, so one can invoke the classic progression: the bedrooms are on the east (which is also, conveniently, the quiet side), and so the living rooms – which are often double-height – can be on the west. The view from the living rooms is towards the square, through the trees and beyond to the Tiergarten. But this view is through the winter garden of the apartment and if it is developed by the tenant as a garden, you will get layers of filtered views.

Housing at the Lutzowplatz, Berlin, 1985 (Peter Cook and Christine Hawley in association with Hinrich and Inken Baller)

So again, with the oversailing bedrooms into the double height and the
general release of space from the
tight side on the east to the loose
side on the west, we have Jekyll and
Hyde, the quiet and the jolly; the
winter gardens themselves trickle
into each other on the side of the
building where it 'all hangs out'. The
repartee is therefore provided by this
straightforward response to the place
and by the different voices of the
different apartments, for only the one-
person flats are directly repeated. In
the end, we liked some apartments
more than others. Unexpected shadows created a particular delight in the
top apartment on the north, which is a
single-height flat but within a barrel
roof. The central cross-corridor is
marked by parallel internal clerestory
glass, and the effect is that the half
light of the opposite end can be seen
over the top . . . we called it the
'railway station' apartment, and the
building workmen themselves would
argue vehemently that it was 'horri-
ble' or the 'greatest'.

It is impossible to compete with the
great 19th century Berlin apartments
without using their great dimensionality, but it *is* possible to talk to the
Berliners with *features of space*.

For many years now, I have been carrying on my own repartee with Frankfurt . . . an old city that seems bent on representing its skyline to imitate, more and more, the city of Houston. Financially and in terms of communication it is an international metropolis, but it is actually a small city: it has many museums and a fantastic cultural programme, but you can walk through it in less than two hours. Frankfurt city is really a core with an explosion of separate 'blobs' thrust out on the countryside. These small towns average around 5,000 to 10,000 each and often end in the word *heim*. They sit in boring flat lands or surrounded by *stadwald*, but never very far from each other. So after a while I thought, 'What would happen if you pulled things together a bit . . . and made Frankfurt into a REAL City?' It involved a lot of mapping, seeding the path for a coagulating action or two. It was helped, of course, by the feel of a place that you have as a pedestrian with several spare evenings on your own and a taste for just strolling around or taking the tram to its terminus 'on spec'. I proposed a system of avenues, that could be flanked by villas: or rather, a variant on the 19th or early 20th-century apartment block of stout and solid

Real City, Frankfurt, 1986

dimensions. The idea was to con-
struct the basic lift shafts and fire
corridors out of cheap concrete-and-
rubbish mix . . . and leave it there. As
hulk. The 'hulk' building can be left
there until someone wants to infill it,
the rows of hulks creating a definite
boulevard scale . . . even though the
gardens might be vegetable patches
and backyard industry is encouraged
in as a constituent part of the city. In
one of the boulevards the 'shed'
version of the hulk is encouraged – so
Frankfurt's tradition of market gardens and workshops is retained in the
Real City that is a metropolis.

The hulks develop . . . and I offer
four or five of my own suggestions of
how: naturally, there is a rather
vegetated one but also another that
looks somewhat like a casbah –
where the screens and balconies
merge together as an endless mesh
between two flats and the outside
world. Other versions are more
dégagé.

I was in Brisbane for a few weeks in the late 1980s and I was intrigued by the 'tin' houses that were built by the English settlers when they found that there were some nasty animals around. They lifted them up on legs and then proved themselves very ingenious with the placing and folding of verandahs, screens, awnings and layered walls. I devised a series of towers that could run alongside Brisbane's downtown with my own reinterpretation of these partis: realising that the preoccupation with complete silhouette and the skin may be logical for high-rise buildings, but has ignored their organic potential. So here, as in Frankfurt, or Oslo (where I have also found a local tradition: that of large wall-lanterns), I am able to bounce off some curious local characteristics. You bring many of your own preoccupations with you, but then you bounce them about with the curiosities. I guess many architects indulge in this form of repartee, but I particularly like the complementary role that is played by the simple and necessary armature: the towers or the hulk frames, a river or a boulevard that act as the pegs off which all these mixtures can play and swirl.

And then the breaking point. A place that you think is simply awful. The *Times* newspaper asked me to make a project for the area behind Waterloo Station in South London. You're confronted with this place, you become appalled and frustrated by it . . . and then . . . 'To hell with it! Let's flood it!' Out of this fascist reaction comes a project that makes an inland bathing lake surrounded by beaches. Towers and mounds and a few remainders of the old South London are also (I suppose) a cry of frustration at the overly protectionist attitude of the English culture of the day.

Towers, Brisbane, 1983

PLAN 12000

SECTION-ELEVATION
AA   1:5

CULTURAL CENTRE

PAVILION

CULTURAL FAN

FREEWAY

CITY FAN

HOVERING FAN

BRISBANE RIVER

MARGARET ST.

PAVILION

LOOP FAN

LOOP BRIDGE

ALICE ST.

A

PARLIAMENT HOUSE

CONVERSATION 6
WALKING AND NARRATIVE

English ideas, which are so often interpreted through English writing create the kind of play or novel which doesn't really have a hero, or a total villain; nor do they necessarily come to a conclusion. In matters of politics or religion or morality, the characters themselves seem to become most telling when they are immoral but also good, wicked but not evil, love-able but with a vicious edge to them . . . so when you come out of the theatre you can ask, (as we did in discussing the architectural criticism) what was it really leading up to? But you also have to admit that there were some marvellous vignettes, some intriguing insights, some unde-veloped pieces of plot, and things going on alongside. The idea of *along-side* can be such a good one, architecturally as well.

Christine Hawley and I entered a competition for the incorporation of an old Carmelite church into a new museum of historic relics (later won and built by Josef Kleihues). A very long ramp was threaded in and out of a series of long chambers (the origi-nal transept and nave, as well as our own additions), and itself would lace around a series of racks, on which the exhibits would rest. The procedure through the museum would therefore be a form of narrative with stops along the way to countenance the pieces – but seeing them in the round and from several different heights and angles, Gothic in spirit as well as space. I hate those museums where you come in and yes, there it is. 'We've got a Picasso, folks, so here it is'. What's left? Some are reasonable buildings, of course, a nice big space . . . 'You've paid your money so go and look in Rooms one to ten'.

Trondheim Library, 1977 (Cook & Hawley)

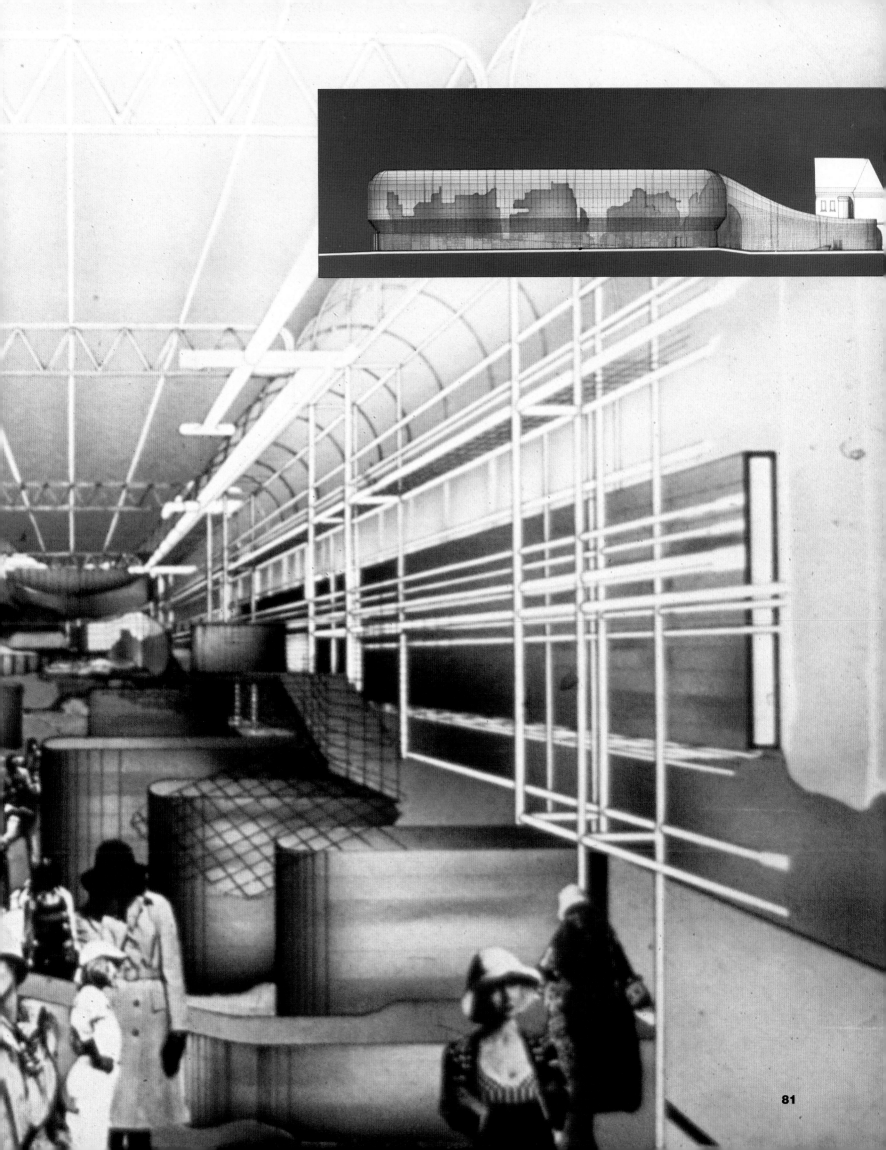

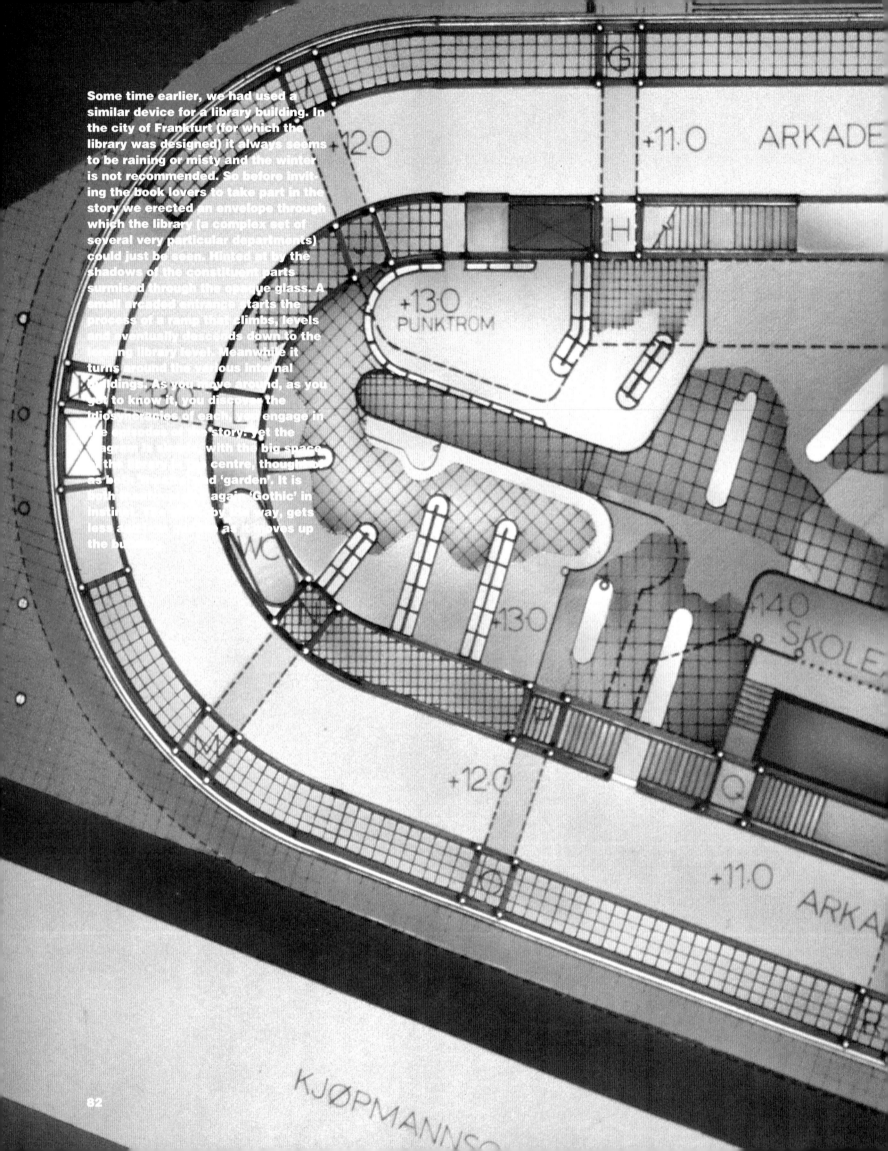

Some time earlier, we had used a similar device for a library building. In the city of Frankfurt (for which the library was designed) it always seems to be raining or misty and the winter is not recommended. So before inviting the book lovers to take part in the story we erected an envelope through which the library (a complex set of several very particular departments) could just be seen. Hinted at by the shadows of the constituent parts surmised through the opaque glass. A small arcaded entrance starts the process of a ramp that climbs, levels and eventually descends down to the leading library level. Meanwhile it turns around the various internal buildings. As you move around, as you get to know it, you discover the idiosyncracies of each, you engage in the collective of the story: yet the diagram is held with this big space at the symbolic centre, thought of as both 'forum' and 'garden'. It is sophisticated but again 'Gothic' in instinct. The library, by the way, gets less and less frantic as it moves up the building.

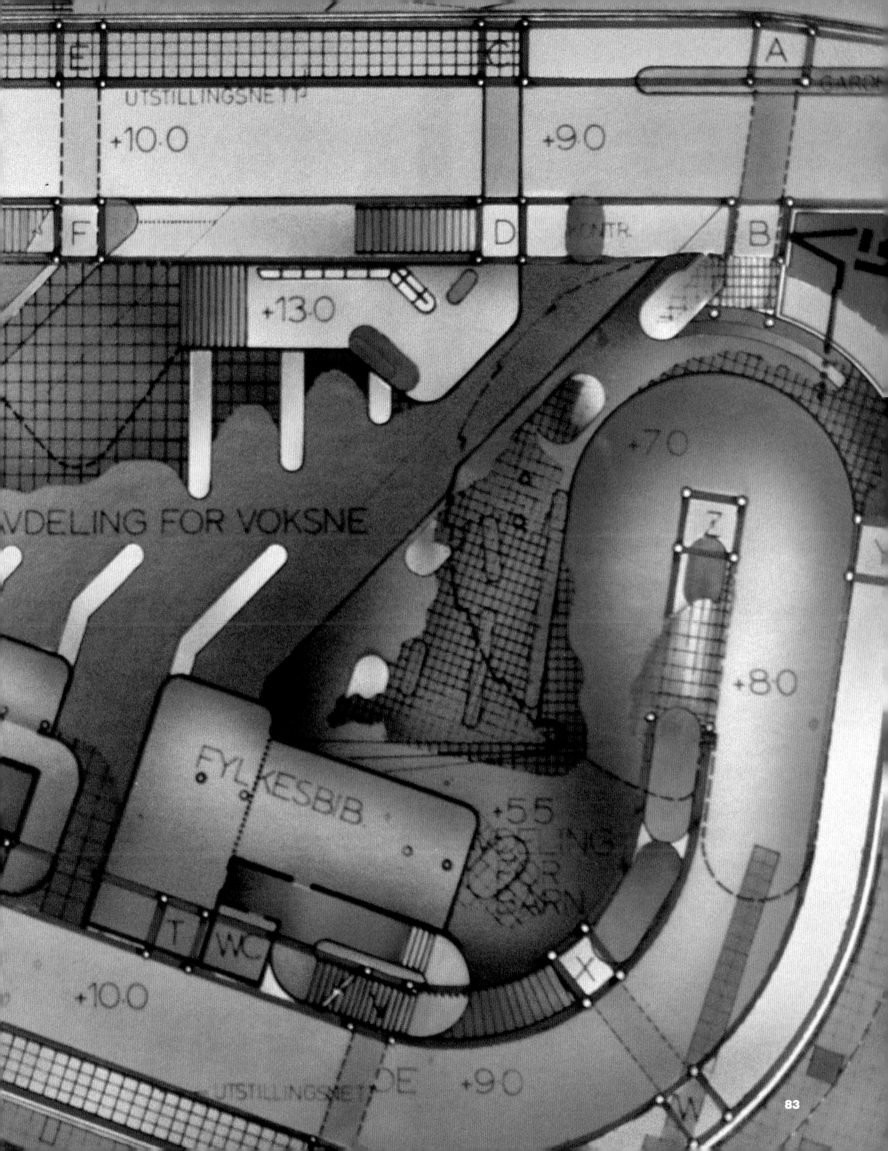

Together with Ron Herron, we made a
scheme for Hamburg which is even
more to do with walking and incidents
along the way. We contrived a thing
called a 'Land-pier'. Hamburg is after
all a port, and part of the designing
was made by the River Elbe where
there is still plenty of real shipping
activity. Our pier starts by the water
and then climbs up and around the
parkland that marks the site of the
old city ramparts. You start to attach
your own episodic bits and pieces,
pause to walk around the giant

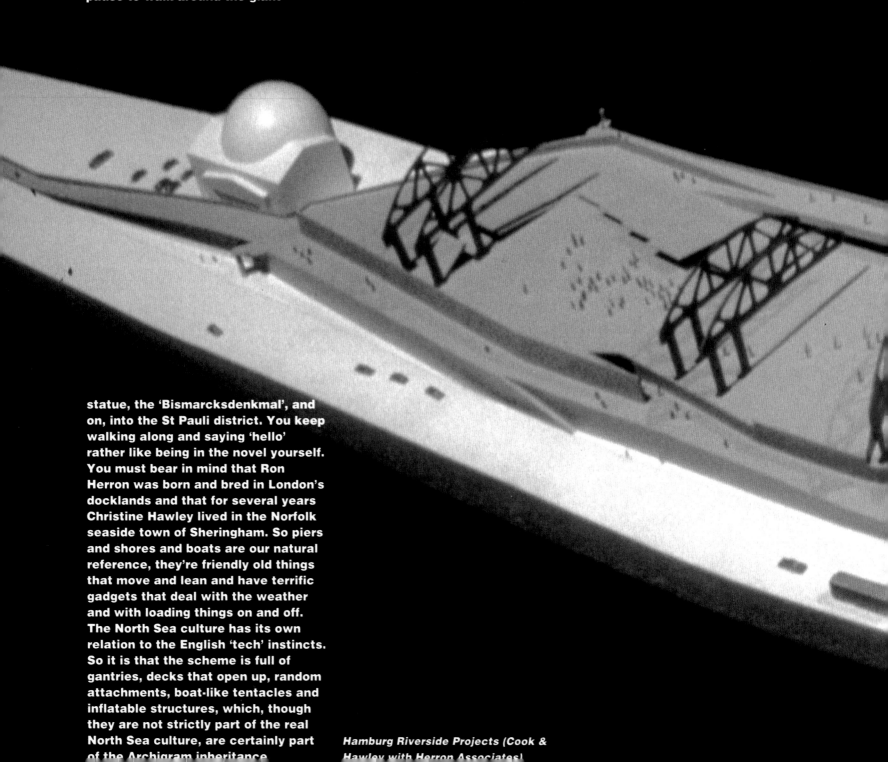

statue, the 'Bismarcksdenkmal', and
on, into the St Pauli district. You keep
walking along and saying 'hello'
rather like being in the novel yourself.
You must bear in mind that Ron
Herron was born and bred in London's
docklands and that for several years
Christine Hawley lived in the Norfolk
seaside town of Sheringham. So piers
and shores and boats are our natural
reference, they're friendly old things
that move and lean and have terrific
gadgets that deal with the weather
and with loading things on and off.
The North Sea culture has its own
relation to the English 'tech' instincts.
So it is that the scheme is full of
gantries, decks that open up, random
attachments, boat-like tentacles and
inflatable structures, which, though
they are not strictly part of the real
North Sea culture, are certainly part
of the Archigram inheritance.

*Hamburg Riverside Projects (Cook &
Hawley with Herron Associates)*

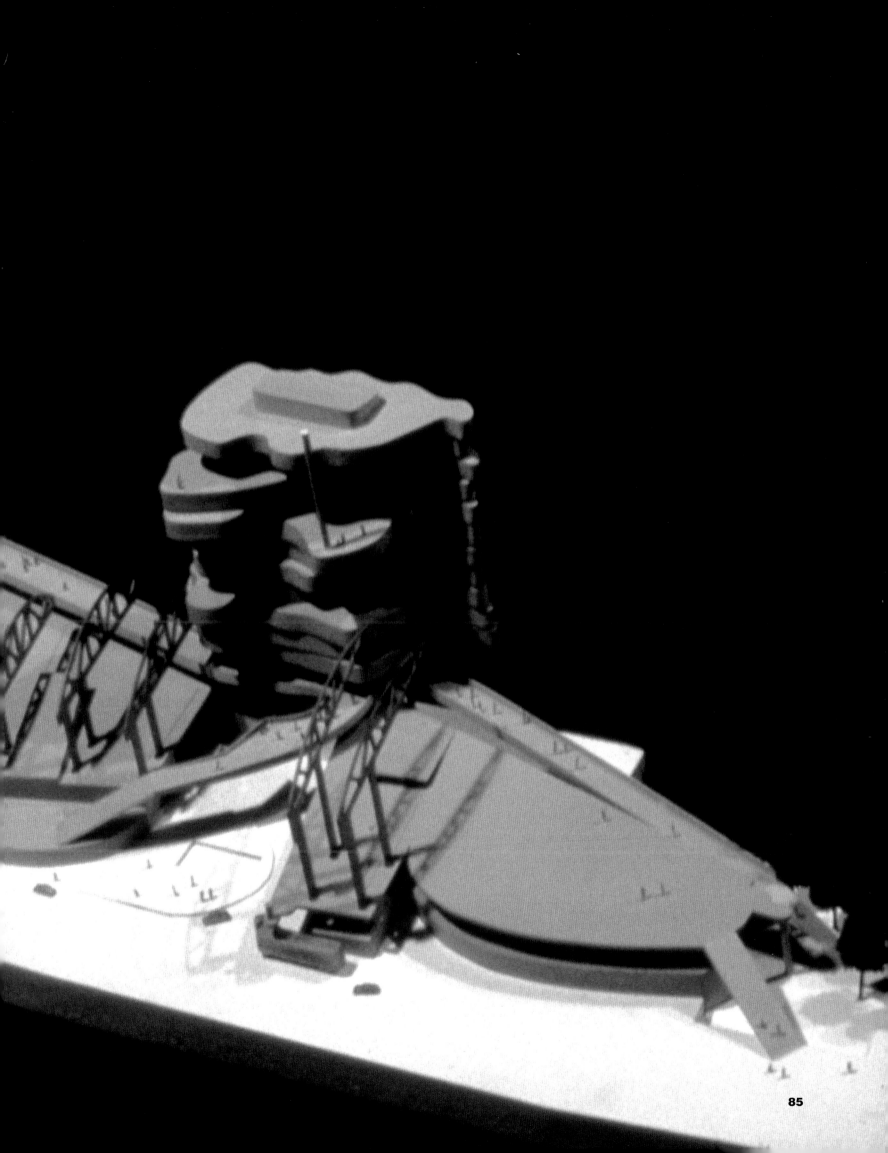

SÜDANSICHT / SCHNITT A-A

HOTEL

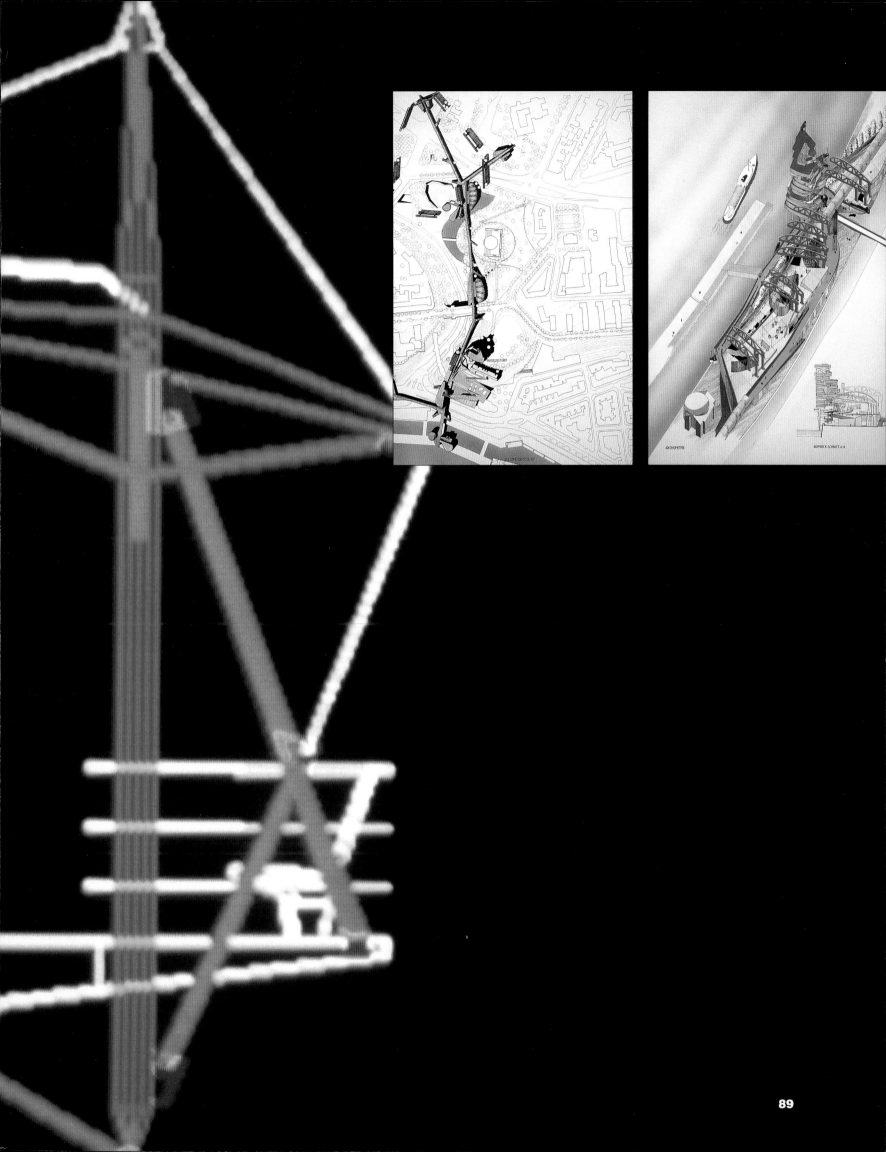

Once you have control over a space, rather than a park (as in Hamburg) you engage in the process of coercion of concentration. You beckon, encourage – then release. You have even more involvement with the recipient than the writer of the play. But first of all, lull them into a calm expectancy. As in Osaka, where our folly for the Garden Expo of 1990 was a quiet metal mask, with a small yellow wand that occasionally made small, twitching movements. And then, suddenly, 'WHOOSH!' This mask erupts into a large splash of water. Then calm returns. You climb up and enter, turn through a black tunnel and turn into a glass chamber rising to a point. Water spills down either side and you can look through to the lake, round which you have been walking for maybe 20 minutes. This time, however, you are looking at it through the distortion of the water on the window so that (perhaps) Turner's distortion of the obvious is invoked. Water seen through water and over water . . . for the floor is a metal grille above the draining water coming down the sides of the chamber. So it is only after moving on and starting to descend out that you see the significance of the splash: for all the draining water is collecting in a hopper that every one and a half minutes tips and thrusts out its load towards the unsuspecting passer-by. Any stylisation of the thing is merely a mask, followed by the wrapping of these events in black anonymous material or in glass. The shape of it is in no category or particular formation: but the interior is very precise. Perhaps if built, our other work would end up in this way?

Folly, Osaka, Expo 1990 (Cook & Hawley)

So much has it become a preoccupation, that walking and wrapping,
episode-making and folding was the
procedure adopted on the largest
project that Cook and Hawley has
ever designed. It was for a combination of World Trade Centre, hotel and
housing and is within sight of our
Berlin-Lutzowplatz building. It has a
very deliberate and complete 'footprint' and this, which perhaps resembles a pair of boomerangs is strong
enough to wrap two controlled open
spaces. Then the whole thing is sliced
by a path that has crossed the
Lanwehrkanal and would continue on
to cross some streets and go directly
into the Tiergarten.

   Christine and I are not given to
'shape' concepts, but were very keen
to define the site and set up a discipline for the scheme. Keen to avoid
that English spillage that often occurs
on large schemes, we spent a lot of
time honing and stroking the shapes
until they were right. Then cast a
great fan of glass onto the ground
level, contained by the hotel and the
long, slicing path. Within the 'glass
ground' would be the shopping and
banking centre. Above the café terraces again the idea of hints and
translucency. From within, a trace of
the world above that can be PEERED
AT. The buildings themselves are
double-skinned, with sensuous cleav-
ages between the inner and the outer.
Much use of glass partitions and
internal skins. Paths weaving gently
round the contours of the space,
terraces and folded ground. A ship-
like strip of 200 flats along the water-
side. A hotel with funky outcrops. A
Berlin aesthetic that is (we thought)
urbane and somewhat International
and contained territory that is as
much in the tradition of the 'resort' as
of the business world. Once again,
many 'walks' and theatrical events
woven into the thing.

World Trade Centre, Berlin, 1991
(Cook & Hawley)

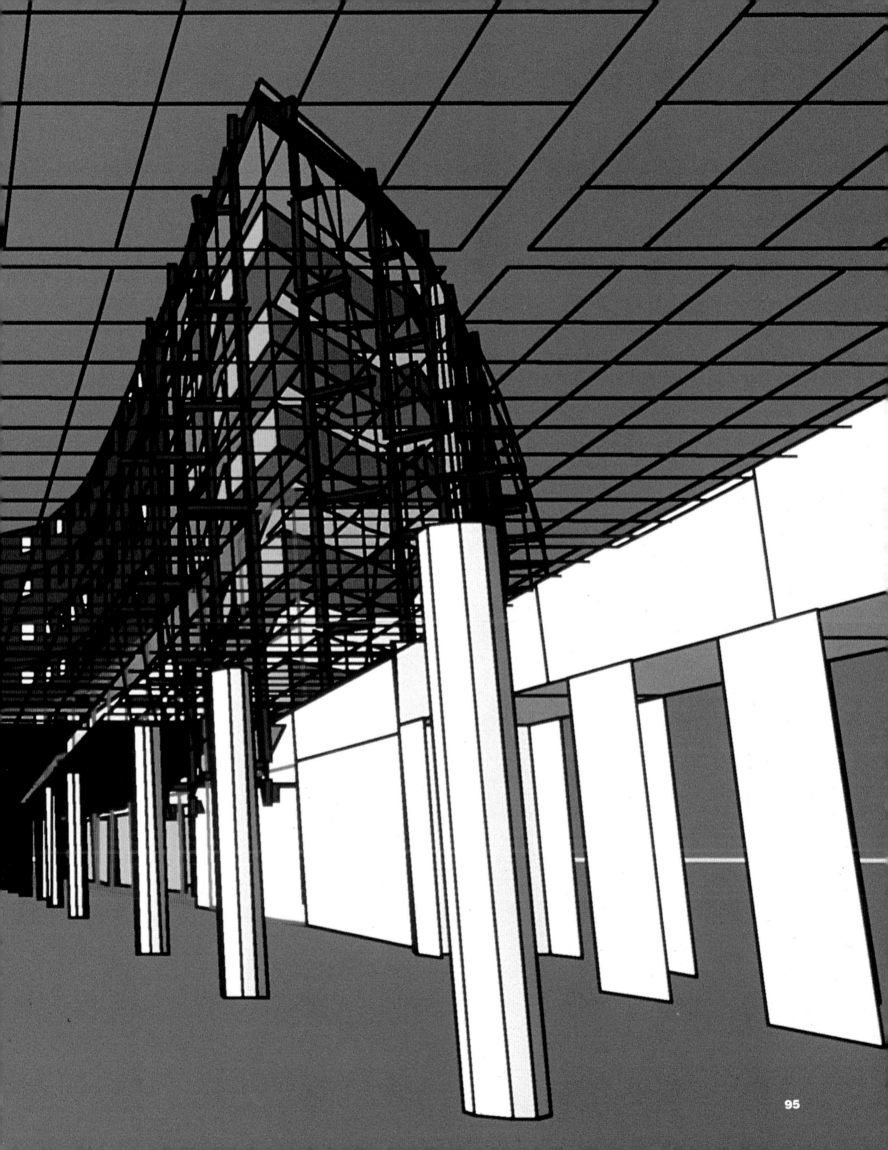

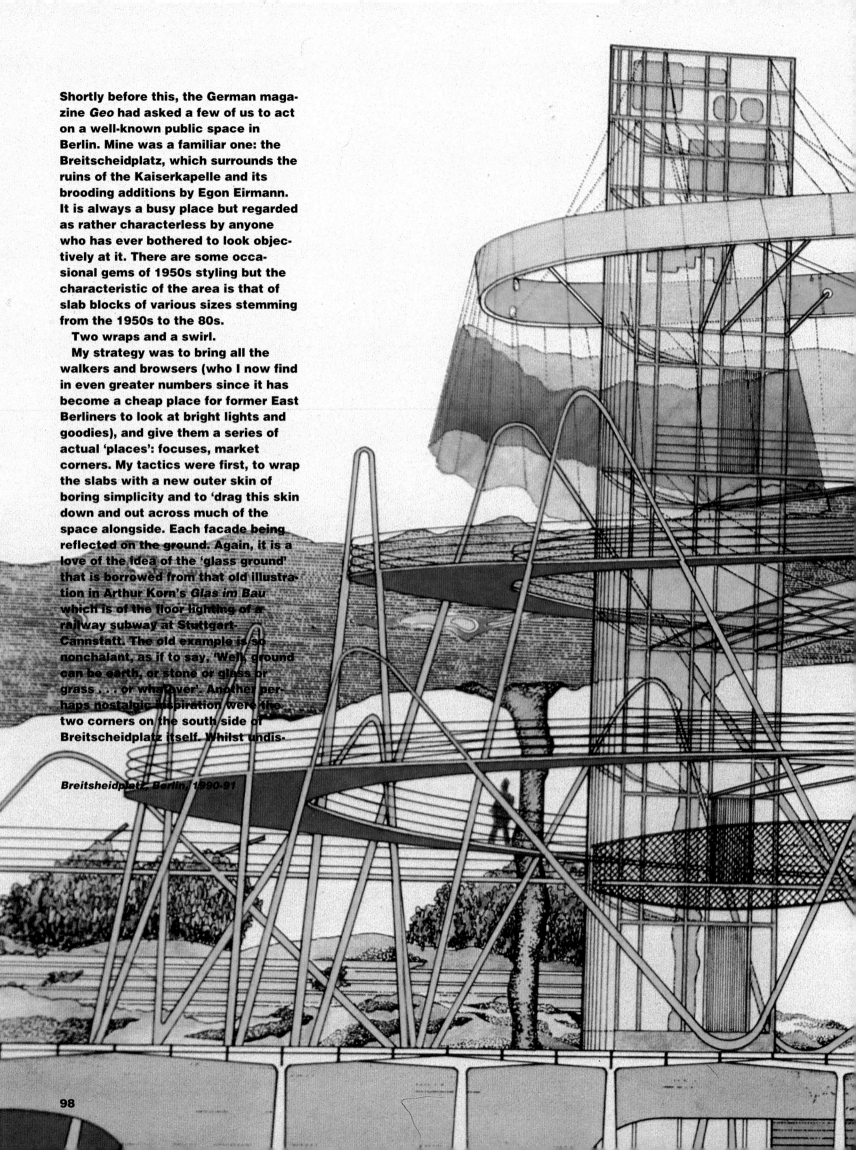

Shortly before this, the German magazine *Geo* had asked a few of us to act on a well-known public space in Berlin. Mine was a familiar one: the Breitscheidplatz, which surrounds the ruins of the Kaiserkapelle and its brooding additions by Egon Eirmann. It is always a busy place but regarded as rather characterless by anyone who has ever bothered to look objectively at it. There are some occasional gems of 1950s styling but the characteristic of the area is that of slab blocks of various sizes stemming from the 1950s to the 80s.

Two wraps and a swirl.

My strategy was to bring all the walkers and browsers (who I now find in even greater numbers since it has become a cheap place for former East Berliners to look at bright lights and goodies), and give them a series of actual 'places': focuses, market corners. My tactics were first, to wrap the slabs with a new outer skin of boring simplicity and to 'drag this skin down and out across much of the space alongside. Each facade being reflected on the ground. Again, it is a love of the idea of the 'glass ground' that is borrowed from that old illustration in Arthur Korn's *Glas im Bau* which is of the floor lighting of a railway subway at Stuttgart-Cannstatt. The old example is so nonchalant, as if to say, 'Well, ground can be earth, or stone or glass or grass . . . or whatever'. Another perhaps nostalgic inspiration were the two corners on the south side of Breitscheidplatz itself. Whilst undis-

Breitscheidplatz, Berlin, 1990-91

tinguished stylistically, they have a great spirit in them because they are both great semi-circular sweeps: not just rounded corners but sweeps of an urban scale (can Mendelsohn's 'Universum' have been their inspiration?). So there's the trick. I can take off from these and start to introduce some more sweeps of my own. The sweeps are the natural focusing points and can absorb small events and markets, but they are primarily the system of drawing up the walkers onto a higher level of bridges that run freely around the open platz.

From this basic equipment of rectilinear glass faces and swirling lines there is the need for only one more ingredient: deliberately a naughty and ungainly one – perhaps 'son of Way Out West', a lurching and usually modest lumpen or sausage-like creature that slips around the edges and may, who knows, anticipate a later version of the scheme. Such a set of performers can be staged by such an entrepreneurial old city.

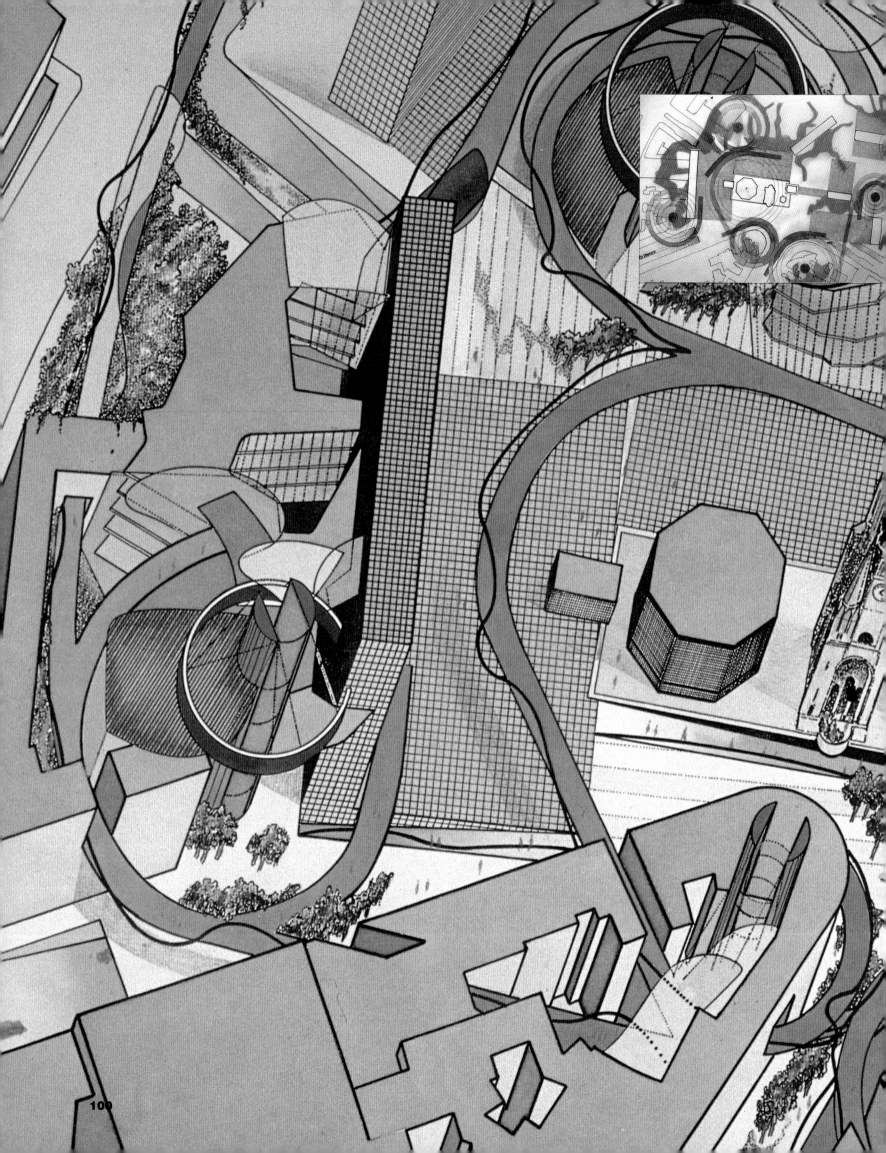

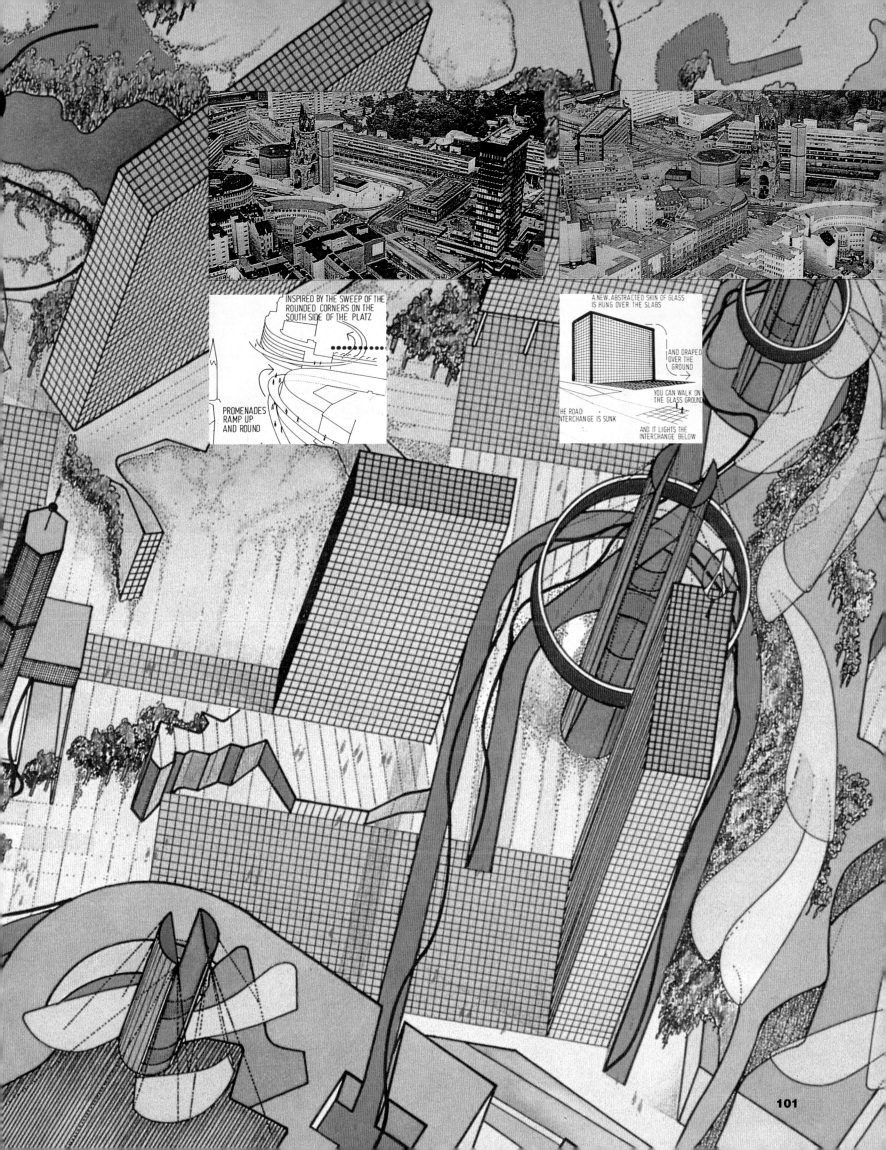

INSPIRED BY THE SWEEP OF THE ROUNDED CORNERS ON THE SOUTH SIDE OF THE PLATZ

PROMENADES RAMP UP AND ROUND

A NEW, ABSTRACTED SKIN OF GLASS IS HUNG OVER THE SLABS

AND DRAPED OVER THE GROUND

YOU CAN WALK ON THE GLASS GROUND

THE ROAD INTERCHANGE IS SUNK

AND IT LIGHTS THE INTERCHANGE BELOW

In the end, though, more perambulations reside in my memory, both recent and long, in lower Hampstead than any other place. Some of these have been undertaken in the (many) parts of the year when it is misty or damp in London. The whole area is a mixture of levels of gentility. On the Hampstead Hill lived intellectuals in earlier times and these now tend to live on the lower slopes. I myself live right at the bottom in a red brick area of tall houses with long gardens. Hampstead is also the source of many watercourses. So damp and red is all around. It is rarely a damp of hard rains and vicious winds . . . it is insidious, fungoid, given to the creation of green stains and the encouragement of moss. On the hill are a number of cottage-like studios and villas. Below lies a large tract of railway land. Not yet quite as brooding as that one in Berlin, but having a tradition of being the backyard of the whole area.

We live in damp, so why not make architecture of the damp? Why not devise a proud urban architecture that can leap over space and create undercrofts where all sorts of random and parasite buildings can nest. Many of these will be backyard industry, studios, workshops, greenhouses, perhaps even small banana plantations – who knows? The main structures will of course house apartments, with as much variety as possible within. On the north, almost no expression, on the south let it all hang in or out. The water is caught in giant hoppers sailing over the roof. It is also piped in from the natural springs as a top-up. It can then gradually be trickled down the south side of the building, via shallow trays and carefully scratched channeling in the wall. The trays can be grilled-over (as we did at Osaka) and the whole thing start to take on its essential patina. Calling the scheme 'Dampstead' becomes inevitable!

There is a steady march of these triangles across from the hilltop area to the railway. The tops remain constant and the bottoms emerge. You can walk in amongst, alongside, or occasionally make contact below. The grain of this part of London is complex. The water will weave on an even smaller trajectory. Each actor his own pace.

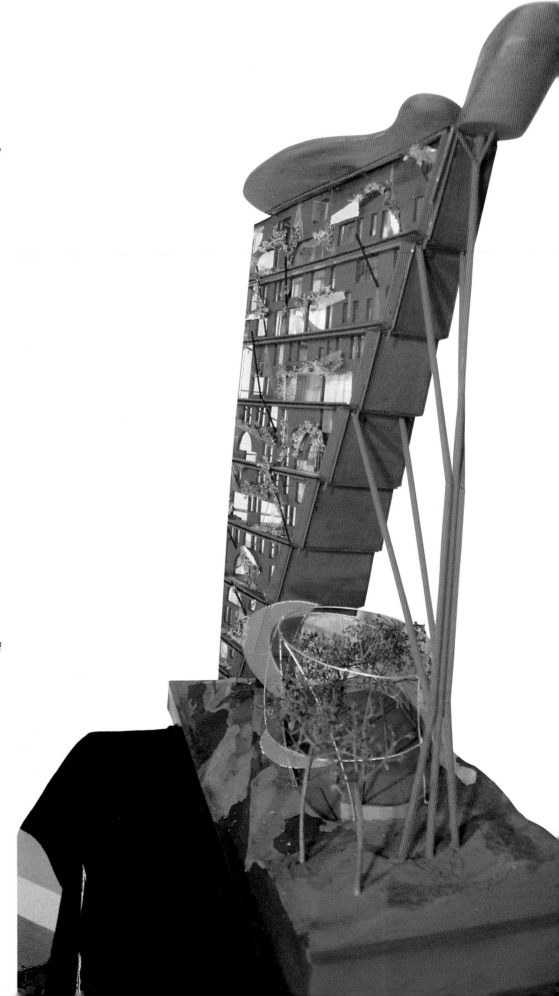

This question of urban grain and the possibility of combining the notion of 'layering' with that of building control (by which I mean the issue of primary structure, paths, grain or lines of force) forms the basis of 'Finchley Road 2'. This assumes, by now, the role of the Dampstead project as 'Finchley Road 1' in a hidden agenda by which I shall propose a series of interferences with the bland progress of that highway.

In Finchley Road 2, the activity of the area, (which is more speculative than entrepreneurial since it is the product of musicians, writers, academics and people with curious sets of expertise) has to be the lifeblood of the scheme. Moreover, I constantly have this instinct for genuine mixed-use in a large city. Why commute? Why not walk past an open window with someone doing a very curious or different task on your way to the video shop?

Those 'swathes' in the Layer city, those crawling sausages at Breitscheidplatz, those gently climbing paths in the Museum in the Sky give me a groundbase for the scheme. Walking and combining purposefulness with overt busibodiness is the stuff of cities. This part of London can handle the condition of intense urbanity which involves the small of the boulangerie and the creaking of the dance studio, the sudden emergence of a home-built racing car with the delicateness of the private psychiatric clinic . . . all in one building. Something that is quite common in Paris or Helsinki, but that we should continue to investigate in London.

Finchley Road 2, 1992

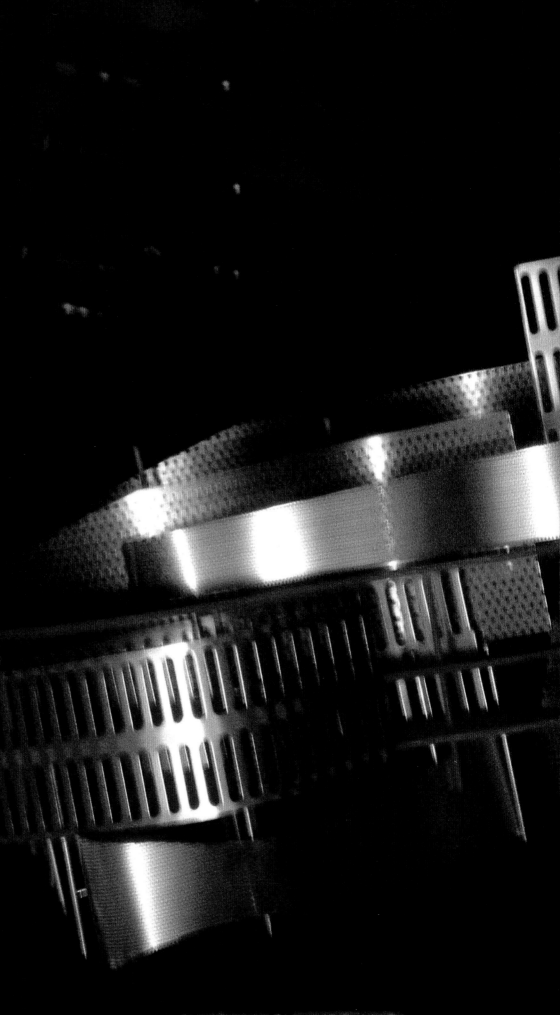

TOWARDS A SYNTHETIC SUBURBIA
Synopsis

THE ENGLISH SCENE – OPEN – GENTLE – LIBERAL – WITHOUT DOGMA a tradition open to many cultures and philosophies . . . against a soft, reassuring background of green grass, gently rolling hills, with very few mountains, and thatched cottages nestling against the asbestos cottages . . . all very much the same . . .
allowing . . .
ameliorating: with gentle argument, with a tolerant (or is it Machiavellian) absorbance of the new and the eccentric into the liberal mainstream . . .

THERE IS EVEN A TRADITION OF ENGLISH ECCENTRICITY:
no wonder that there is open conversation here about possibilities . . . but little actually *happens*
open . . . tolerant . . . cloying?
a trap?
an indulgence?
might we all return to pretty, tiny, English picturesqueness

REMEMBER ARCADIA . . .
Victorians who invented their way out of almost anything . . . Men of spirit, wit, unencumbered by paranoia

GREEN GRASS, GENTLY ROLLING HILLS, WILL THEY SMOTHER THE CRIES OF THE ECOSTRATEGISTS AS THEY SMOTHERED THE INFANT MODERN MOVEMENT IN ARCHITECTURE?
or doesn't it matter

ARCHIGRAM
ARCHIGRAM HOT
ARCHIGRAM NATURAL
ARCHIGRAM TECHNICAL
ARCHIGRAM HEADY
ARCHIGRAM SWEATY
ARCHIGRAM UNINHIBITED
ARCHIGRAM INVENTIVE

ARCHIGRAM DEVIL-MAY-CARE

such an explosion was inevitable in the face of the slowness and tranquillity of the English scene?

ARCHIGRAM ANARCHIC
ARCHIGRAM A-POLITICAL
ARCHIGRAM OPPORTUNISTIC
ARCHIGRAM OPEN-ENDED . . . (but here a clue maybe not so un-English after all?)

ARCHIGRAM BRASH
ARCHIGRAM STYLED AND SEDUCTIVE
ARCHIGRAM AS AN ALTERNATIVE

ARCHIGRAM ANTI-ARCHITECTURE . . . but . . .
ARCHIGRAM MAKING ARCHITECTURE . . . its **ALL** the same
NOW YOU SEE US – NOW YOU DON'T
Stop trying to pin it down you boring architectural historians . . . The Italians may like to send up a fog of literO-politicO reasonings
BUT BASICALLY THERE ARE MORE WAYS OF COOKING AN EGG . . .
A SYNTHESIS?
IT COULD BE . . .

a preoccupation with change leads to a preoccupation with metamorphosis
a preoccupation with change leads to the idea of infiltration

110

a preoccupation with replacement leads to alternatives
alternatives lead to absorption of the old into the new . . . the new into the old

ARCHIGRAM INVENTING
ARCHIGRAM QUAINT
ARCHIGRAM TOLERANT

the idea of a **QUIETLY TECHNOLOGISED FOLK – SUBURBIA . . .**
analyse that: **QUIETLY . . .** gently, gradually, unrhetorically, **TECHNOLOGISED . . .** systematised, invention-ridden, **FOLK . . .** popular, non-architectonic, cheerful **SUBURBIA . . .** real urbanism that we already have

PROJECTS ON HAND:

MONTE CARLO: the cybernetic magic theatre folded into a mound of ground . . .

HEDGEROW VILLAGE: so quietly technologised that it is the English . . . and characteristically, the pneumatic structure can live with the stone cairn, the do-it-yourself with the Detroit capsule . . .

MAGIC MUSHROOM THEATRE: for our travelling exhibition: the armchair-animal-anenome-bed-instrument-plaything-university-cat

CRATER CITY: the most intense comfort sunk into the hillside 16,000 people in a single building, all in a greenhouse-bunker but you don't see any building

THE URBAN MARK: the megastructure that eats itself away before it comes together but is always together . . .

ORCHARD PLACE: I quote:
The fruit orchard . . . relaxed, acceptable, a megastructure manqué
Let all comers come
. . . as once, free-ranging chickens roamed and pecked
let people roam and make camp

Another kind of orchard . . . an artificial one if you like . . . it has servicing in boxes
and minimum structure: umbrellas from which things can be draped
Alternatively, you can regard it as a conceptual megastructure

With this situation, if we let all comers come . . .
The mind boggles
It might lead to a completely relaxed and casual camping environment

The trees creeping back maybe?

Inevitably . . . an analogy – even a direct connection – can be made between the idea of the gentle
orchard and the hidden service network . . . the Rok-plug and Log-plug sundrome (David Greene)

. . . next?
Gnarled Oak metropolis? A new project for Venice, Calif? The pebble-dash university?

Peter Cook, May 1972

ON BEING ENGLISH

Last night Ron Herron and I gave a lecture. It was held in a large shed in Santa Monica that is infilled with giant scaffolding, steel trusses and brightly painted boards. The whole place is bugged for sound, video cameras whirring and arc lights in your face, for the philosophy of the place – the wildest and most experimental of the West Coast architecture schools – is that the lecture that is in the can (and therefore available for relaxed viewing) is at least as valuable as the platform event itself. I suppose this is an updating of the philosophy that suggests that the beautifully printed catalogue is worthy of much more investment than the exhibition that initiates it, which is noticeable in German or Italian events.

We English sit somewhere else, for to us, the real event is more piquant: the occasional fluffs of speech, the anecdotes, the asides between the speakers and the unexpected arrival of Arata and Aiko Isozaki in the middle of the lecture so that Ron and I could beam a few private jokes their way; these things cannot be captured on tape or predestined in a catalogue. Yet the central space of SCI-ARC is a reminder of Archigram more than anything else. It is the built manifestation of the idea that a place of education is to do with interaction. It uses the miniaturised 'Plug-in City' in the form of scattered carrells for the students, some of them high up in the structure, and presents an attitude of the whole school being open to all the students; I am writing this piece in an open space, necessarily insulated from the comings and goings of the place by my stereo headphones which are at this moment playing me Delius' 'Cello Concerto'.

On reflection, the designs that we made in the mid-1960s did not sufficiently ponder the way in which the individual needs to escape. I can shut my eyes and forget the palm trees and stucco and hazy sun and think of the Yorkshire Moors, then I can open them up again and look out on Santa Monica (incidentally I prefer Santa Monica to the Yorkshire Moors!). We drew very elaborate armatures. We were concerned about the consistency of those armatures. I suspect that the reiteration of the rounded corners (to which all of the capsules subscribed) was as important to the whole Archigram Group as the preference for Suprematist gambits must have

been to the young Russians of 1929, or a certain kind of Ungers window can be recognised in current German competition projects.

In the intervening years, I realise myself just how architectural that work on Plug-in City and Walking City and Computer City really was. The references were simultaneously made towards the space race and car production, but even here we had Buckminster Fuller as a kind of High Priest figure, who had philosophised and even mysticised upon their significance. We were there to give form and substance and that quality of architectural prejudice without which you get, for instance, the hilarity of the interior of the dome house that Fuller built for himself, where nasty little triangular cupboards are only capped by double beds heading for curved walls at high speed. In a sense, Konrad Wachsmann was even more important to us than Bucky. For Wachsmann was a formalist: the sheer aesthetic quality of his designs for intertwining joints tells us where his preferences lie. There is similarly a wilfulness about his giant trusses and his last great designs for the city hall of California City. There is a slab at ground level held there by giant tension cables. This is not just a question of logical structuring, or of resource equations; it is art and contains a tremendous amount of prejudice.

One realises the importance of the tradition of structural innovation that characterises English design. In recent years we have spawned some engineers (Newby, Rice, Hunt) who are in the direct line of descent from the 18th and 19th-century designers of the London railway stations and railway bridges. Take a look at the roof of Frankfurt or Hamburg stations, then compare them with Paddington or Liverpool Street and ponder over that part of the English mind that enjoys fiddling about and twisting and ameliorating substances until they operate at the edge of known methodology – or even beyond it. Even as quite academically trained architects (which we all were), we were as aware of (and excited by) these things as we were by the concurrent activity in the art world; the English pop artists were, some of them, our friends, but the movements really took on separate trajectories. Whereas the artists became more literary and political (Blake,

Hamilton, Tilson) we became more and more affected by the possibilities of science and social patterning. The real significance of the electric car, the TV dinner, the caravan city, the significance of a hundred thousand people on a hilltop, turned on by lights and music: this must – could only – be described as a CITY. So it was that the determinism of Plug-in City (as an aesthetic), or of Walking City (as an object) was replaced in 1969-70 by the Instant City, a nomadic caravan where there is no particular element more important than the other, and where the aesthetic itself has begun to fragment. That the need for a rediscovery of language made itself felt by the mid-1970s is another story. It amazes me, in fact, that the Archigram 'language' grew up as quickly as it did, was as pungent as it was and became as imitable as it was. Of course, the essence of the ideas lay elsewhere. As I have already suggested, the rounded corner was a stylistic label, a metaphor that became a minor device, whereas the craneway was a device that needed to have some metaphorical input added to it.

A stabilising influence was the morality of realism that meant that (wherever possible) we made the projects to the normal dimensions, of the normal materials and (strangely enough) with the normal composition of such things as houses and shops and balconies and staircases. 85 percent of Archigram projects are immediately buildable using current techniques. Indeed, we were (and are) often irritated by so-called 'ideas' architecture that is buildable by an undefined but all-purpose material, or that simply escapes detailed scrutiny by claiming 'conceptual' relevance for drawn objects that have no likelihood of real existence.

We had all spent years making working drawings. Subsequently we have all spent years as teachers. Perhaps the observer can spot this in the designs by Ron Herron, Mike Webb and myself, who constitute the part of Archigram that has (separately) continued making projects. Certainly the subject matter of the projects has that built-in rhetoric that should not be underestimated in the apparently descriptive style of our work.

When we made the 'Living City' exhibition in London's ICA in 1963 (the first combined operation by what became known as the

Archigram Group) we were all too aware of the exhibition 'This is Tomorrow' made by the Independent Group in 1956. Retrospectively, the two events seem close together, yet the gap at the time was quite wide. Mike Webb had been a student of James Stirling, David Greene (briefly) and of Bucky Fuller, while I had studied with Peter Smithson, and the conscious decision to join in with 'us' rather than 'them' was made and stated by Warren Chalk, the oldest member of the group. It is characteristic of a younger syndrome sitting under the shadow of an urbane and productive older syndrome in the same city, that the former should express irritation and frustration with the latter. We felt that after the high jinks and futurism of the Smithsons' 'House of the Future' and the articulation of their Sheffield University project, they were suddenly becoming quiet and drearily rational. So we saw our own capsules and tents and will-o-the-wisp urbanism as a homage to the Smithsons' earlier days. They, in their turn regarded us, as rather hot and sweaty, or as 'Mickey Mouse' architects.

This last term can be pondered as I sit in the city of Mickey Mouse himself and remember that Ron Herron and I made some of our best Instant City images whilst here in 1969. Elsewhere I have written on the changes in Los Angeles during the intervening years, but there is still that quality of invention and juxtaposition that makes for a truly collage city (it is just that Colin Rowe has become too much of an Easterner). In a sense, it is these two aspects of design that have stayed with me since the early Archigram days. One's irritation with some current American or German architecture is not with its stylistic or literary references (which I enjoy myself), but with its sometime 'deadness'; its refusal – or is it ignorance – to develop the potential of all the bits and pieces of a building, or, like the English station roofs, to stretch the fabric. There is this relationship between invention per se and the idea of the 'new', but the buildings of the 19th century in particular seemed to be able to combine scholarship, or nostalgia, or

historicism with the making of new kinds of space, new kinds of element and new detail devices.

It seems that there is now a relaxation towards the idea of megastructures and the notion that a city might well be a dynamic mat upon which other mats might lie. Of course this was the essential concept of Plug-in City and the quality that links it with my current preoccupation – the 'Layer City' – in which the Mesh concepts of 1979-81 are now extended to an urban scale. It makes Los Angeles even more useful as an observable model. It extends the delight with the 'on-off' lights of Las Vegas, the possibility of heroic buildings such as Pelli's Pacific Design Center (the 'blue whale') acting as a mirror for the tacky shacks of West Hollywood, or as a heroic marker for them and subsequently as a part of a larger mesh of heroic monumental buildings (in the sense of the 19th-century institutions of Berlin, London or Paris) that makes some cities into a metropolis. At this point, one realises that we have much in common with the Venturis, though neither would have thought so ten or 15 years ago.

In England, however, we have a culture that has always thrived on overlay and upon a lack of rhetoric that is irritating to those outside. After a thousand years without being invaded, we have a continuous mat of building, we have a 'squirearchy' rather than a series of competitive States. The city of Norwich, where I lived as a child, has two hundred medieval churches. Some of them are silly, some magnificent, some of them are boring. In that city (a prosperous one), the successive generations have brought industrialisation and the invention of marvellous warehouses and factories and regeneration. There has been a discovery of a local aesthetic of brightly coloured buildings and, most recently, the highest of high technology in the form of Norman Foster's Sainsbury Centre for the Arts at the University of East Anglia. At this point we can pause to reflect upon the believed manifestation of Archigram ideas in several buildings that have been

made by Foster and by his friend Richard Rogers. It is no secret that many of their talented younger assistants have been students of Archigram people, and that our relations with these offices are close. So here is a difficult territory upon which to comment since it raises all those classic issues about origin, innovation and the ownership of ideas. It raises also, the more creative discussion about contact between the so-called academic and the 'builder-architect'.

In our teaching, we have deliberately kept slightly nearer the world of real architects – who we like to have on our students' crits – rather than theorists who use these events for advertising their latest book. This may have bracketed us with the many boring pragmatists on the English scene, but that has been a risk worth taking. For, you see, we really wanted to build a Plug-in City. We really know that it is possible for granny to take off into the street in her electric-powered armchair. It is really funny to see some of the Japanese attempts at capsule towers and Norwegian attempts at megastructures and American attempts at internalised cities. They always get it too static, too glossy and even the Centre Pompidou gets it too consistent.

I have seen the beginnings of Archigram Revival architecture: at Liverpool (where none of us have any connections) as well as the AA in London, which as everyone knows, is the most anticipatory of schools.

What are we going to do about this? As Ron Herron prepares to build delightful simulator machines in the English Midlands and I prepare to build an elegant (but solar) blue villa on a German hillside, how can we explain that the big stalks and hanging cables may be nice, but are no use at all if the concept of the city is stiff, the opportunism of the parts is dead and the people within cannot write a short piece of reflective prose without their Walkman being on?

Text for Daidalos *Magazine, Berlin, written at SCI-ARC, Southern California Institute for Architecture, Santa Monica, March 23, 1981*

THE SHADOW HOUSE

The idea of a piece of architecture that is infinite rather than finite is constantly tempting us. Instinctively, this has lain behind a whole trail of projects: the metamorphosis of the Urban Mark (Cook 1972), the transience of the 5-Minute House (Hawley 1975), and the 'will-o-the-wisp' quality of the various mesh projects – the Trondheim Library (1977), the Meshed Ground (Hawley 1978) and the structure that we are now building at Linz – the 'Forum Design – Geschwindigkeit und Information' pavilion.

We are inspired by the notion that spaces need not be defined by walls. Lines need not be boundaries. Objects seen may be both illusory and tangible, or an elusive object might be related to something that is tangible and tactile, but not too obviously.

We suspect that paths might contain the conditions of maximum experience; leading onwards in a series of conditions, always unfolding. And paths might have a more implicit content than those set pieces that we call 'rooms'. Perhaps the analogy here is that of the wayward English narrative that unwinds from incident to incident in anticipation of the gradual understanding of the total situation by the accumulation of clues. By contrast with the continental insistence on thesis, polemic, or the theatre of the set piece, there is no stated conclusion.

We are, however, conscious all the time of the need for a programme. We need, and we use those armatures of regulation that can set off the process, whether it be kinetic, tabloid or substantive. In such a piece of architecture, this role will be played by objects and arrangements that have a primary definition: the axes, the structure, the most recognisable objects, the most iconographic objects. But then it is our wish to treat such aristocrats amongst the community of parts as irreverently as we dare; to taunt them, defile them, sully them, and turn some into mere ghosts of themselves.

Amongst a collection of immediately buildable houses such objectives might seem irrelevant? Yet to us, any discontinuity between 'buildable' architecture and 'conceptual' architecture is unthinkable – there is always a back-and-forth traffic, and the middle ground is, perhaps, the most fascinating. Hence, the 'Meshed Ground' project and the Linz pavilion are merely versions of the same building, and similarly, the quite functional Trondheim Library has been feeding our more abstract work conspicuously for the last three years.

Trondheim's parent, and perhaps also the parent of the Shadow House, is the house on the Via Appia (1976). It was concerned with an architecture of disintegration; the ways in which paths and zones can coalesce into an atmosphere, and then melt away again, rather than depend upon 'rooms'. Its defining paths were defined by the presence of ruins that were challenged by the deliberate newness of the architecture, yet it was ultimately to join them as a kind of relic in its own right, by way of its disintegrity. It also offers a clue to the present project in its concern with retaining an ambiguity towards its line of enclosure.

The Shadow House stands between the city street (to the south), the Rock (to the west), the open countryside (to the north) and a series of gardens (to the east). Each of these places its own pressures upon the house, to which it can respond. It can draw aspects of each into itself, it can send out a signal towards them, or it can bed itself into them. The programme demands a central axis; the formal route from city to country. The house sends out a hand (or is it a debased Tempietto?) towards the city street. At the other end this is echoed by a slightly wayward colonnade that introduces itself to the meadow.

A more divergent route climbs up the Rock; it is in fact a sly path up to the bedroom pavilions. The inhabitants of the house each have a suite that is private – virtually a salon in itself. It commences with a stepped boudoir – perhaps in the tradition of the actor's dressing-room (in social terms); beyond is a water-room – more private and more indulgent; beyond this is the bedchamber. The suite has constantly changing and flickering light, and very small, localised prisms and their attendant shadows abetted by the water falling past from the Rock.

To the east lie the public stages, terracing up from the water garden that lies between them and the street. The fragmentary nature of this garden is misleading, for it contains scrambled vestiges of a formal, radial plan and it rapidly starts to coalesce into the 'kitchen' stage, where the clusters of appliances recall the stones amongst the water. In their case, the thin slivers of light form the necessary streams.

As the stages rise towards those places where more self-conscious social games can be played, the surrounding architecture becomes more and more intangible: merely a web of filters and screens. There are objects that perhaps move, or are merely shadows of objects elsewhere, or shadows that suggest the possible presence of objects. The northern edge of the building is a skin, but one that progresses round from the Rock – where it is sharp and aggressive – towards the gardens, with an ever-increasing waywardness. It diverges to become two skins that eventually involve the garden itself. Indeed, there is eventually no identifiable division between the garden and the house, as there has not been between the cascade of the water and the solid paths, or the structure and the filtering elements.

The house is a rotating mesh with paths that link (as from the pavilions to the stages), that wind (as from the axis to the stages), that climb (onto the stages, the roofs, the rock) and that delve (into the unknown).

Life is played out amongst these meshes and temptations. In the end, it sustains the confrontation of the city with the Rock (perhaps a symbol of 'hard' building, the definition of the rock by the meadow, the contrast of the meadow with the garden, and the assertion of the garden over the city) in pointing to the inevitable melting of each of these adversaries into the next.

Peter Cook, 1981

THE BEACH HOUSE

During the process of designing the Blue house, for the 'chain house' category in the Landstuhl competition, Christine Hawley had produced a large, straddling villa, with the semicircular part backed by a diagonal and then by a 'streetside' wing. This was edited out, as it contravened the site requirements. Nonetheless we both remained very fond of the scheme, and after the competition, welcomed the opportunity to re-examine it, on a site that I knew well from my Bournemouth days.

Both of us had spent childhoods living by the sea and the deep-seated association of that stream of modern architecture is inspired by sun, air, breeze and the various analogies of beach-houses, boats, decks and the free nature of seaside life, which had for me a special significance in my early training. During my first two years as a student at Bournemouth, I was taught by an old architect, Jasper Salwey, who it was known, had had an eccentric career. Only many years after his death, I was told that the series of modern white houses, the Palace Court hotel, and most of the rest of the buildings that were Bournemouth's contribution to the spread of 'modern', 'moderne' or even 'art deco' architecture, had been designed by Salwey, hired job-by-job.

These buildings had always held a romance for me and, even after years of the Smithsons, Le Corbusier, or Archigram, I returned to them with considerable respect.

The Blue house/Beach house examines the proposition of a two-generation family. The older members have the forward pavilion centring on the large volume and are able to retreat into their study balconies, while the younger members are based in the games room and the boardwalk. This walk develops from the small, more sheltered garden court down, progressively, to beach level. The progress is marked by a pergola that is both a fixture for the garden plants and flowers, and, in a more stripped-down form, for the deck activities.

The rear pavilion, mainly bedrooms, is related to the Yellow house, and the games room is part of the Via Appia/Arcadia City family of dug-in rooms that have a skin-to-solid roof progression. It is in the Bournemouth/Mediterranean/Los Angeles mode: an outward house that hugs the descent of the sand-dune that forms the Sandbanks peninsula at the entrance to Poole Harbour.

Peter Cook, 1981

THE KARMELITERKIRCHE, FRANKFURT
Museum of Antiquities

Of the six cities that have tried, since the war, to replace Berlin as West Germany's fulcrum, Frankfurt is the one that is most disliked by sensitive foreigners. It has become a cliché to describe the outcrop of tower blocks in the banking area as an American city that just happens to be in Europe. Its role as a point of interchange – 'the ford of the Franks' – since before Roman times has been developed by successive generations of merchants and travellers and is now endorsed by the existence of Europe's third most international airport. So it is a place which people pass through quickly, preferring not to glance, and head onward to a pretty Austrian valley, to the remaining, shadowy tantalisation of Berlin, or to change planes for Venezuela.

Statistically, it probably suffered no more war damage than Cologne or Hamburg, but Frankfurt's buildings of the 1950s and 1960s are even more bland than theirs. In the 1920s and 1930s a strong political motivation enabled Ernst May (the city architect) to build some of the brightest and most imaginative peoples' housing. The various projects involved Mart Stam and JJP Cud and Ferdinand Kramer, who is still active enough to join us on a student jaunt around town. Yet it is now very markedly lacking in any local architectural practices of note, especially by comparison with Stuttgart where there is an almost Milanese feeling of being surrounded by 'over-design'. Similarly, there are far fewer art galleries than in Düsseldorf, Munich or Cologne, and no really famous symphony orchestra. Even the annual book fair does not seem to create anything more than a glancing – a circumstantial – presence.

Christine, as a regular visiting academic, has nonetheless found herself using the place as a working, socialising, optimistic visitor and since we started to interchange students between the AA and the Staedelschule (the art academy with a small architectural department) there has been some reason for us to look beyond an easy categorisation and prejudice.

We found that there had, in fact, been quite a strong cultural milieu before the war, but very largely Jewish. The Staedelschule has continued as a major studio for Germans and Austrians and now houses not only Johannes Schreiter (probably the greatest living stained glass artist), but also Peter

Kubelka, the originator of Structuralist film-making and Gunther Nitsch, the outrageous Viennese actionist who cuts open his own flesh as part of his art work. There are even strong rumours that Frankfurt will woo Josef Beuys away from his loved-hated Cologne; for the city has acknowledged its need for culture and as one of the world's richest cities it can afford to buy it.

Along the River Main sit a series of museums. Some are in old merchants' villas and others in purpose-built buildings of the late 19th century. It is very pleasant and the 'American' city is seen across the river from the Museumplein as a detached – almost abstracted – entity. Amazingly, the city is building seven new museums; collecting collections of archives, remains, postage stamps and architectural drawings. Oswald Matthias Ungers is the architect who will convert the interior of a massive villa into the Deutsches Architektur Museum for which the new collection already includes the work of Mies van der Rohe, Robert Venturi and some current AA personalities.

The latest in the series of museums have (probably for political reasons) been the subject of architectural competitions, and the city's cultural director was urged by Ungers, and by Heinrich Klotz (author of Conversations with Architects and director designate of the Architektur Museum) to invite as participants a series of non-German architects whose work will be familiar to all current students and Post-Modernists. So it was fascinating to watch the squeals of embarrassment of the German architects who were totally outclassed by Richard Meier (First prize) and Venturi-Rauch-Scott-Brown and Hans Hollein (Second prizes) in the competition for the Historical Museum.

When we were 'invited' to take part in the next round, for the Museum of Antiquities, we were well aware of the implicit politics; of a likely ricochet effect if another group of foreigners swept the board and of the possibility that the last of the series might never get built anyway, now that Germany too is feeling the pinch. We realised that a project which involves the partial refurbishment of an old lump of building along with a knitting operation for the new part of the structure is itself a special task demanding a certain kind of patience and avoidance of

bombast. The Karmeliterkirche is one of the few really ancient structures left in the downtown area. This is characteristic of a city that grew randomly, opportunistically and by a constant layering process. Indeed, a look at the map and a meander through the back of the town gives a feeling of familiarity to an Englishman. Since Frankfurt was a merchants' city, there were no palaces or ceremonial ways, no vistas created for the enjoyment of a prince. A bunch of Carmelite monks would have had to carve out a church and a cloister as best they could, against some old town walls and, as their fortunes improved, to cobble together the odd aisle or the odd apse in a tough – almost rough-and-ready – gothic manner. So the choice of this building was slightly strange – itself partially circumstantial and partially emotional. The housing of historic remnants could be associated with the rebuilding of one of the few pieces of genuine Gothic in the city. Too bad that it is not along the museum strip, but it is within the medieval walls, almost within the old Roman town, and almost (though irritatingly not) by the side of the river. The cloister itself (rebuilt) is as delightful as any in Oxford. The surrounding roads are a quiet backwater within the 'American' city. What is needed is a building of spirit without rhetoric. A gothic building perhaps.

Three years before, we had designed a building in an old downtown area of Trondheim in Norway and had similarly pondered over the degree to which a cultural building can be regarded as just another piece of typical urban grain, or whether it has to spell out its offering to the populus. The earlier building was for a library. This was to be for a museum. Both times we had strong views about the potential of a building type that is a hangover of the 19th century, when a city's beneficence was marked by the ostentatious provision of such facilities, along with a concert hall, public baths and a town hall clock. If we could post-rationalise the 20th-century need for information retrieval and the Nordic need for physical comfort, then here in Frankfurt we felt the need to explode the heavy and static tradition of the museum.

If the tradition of Gothic architecture includes daring structural innovation and dramatic conditions of light, shade and view, then it seems also to suggest the qualities of theatre and enlivenment that could mark a progressive museum. A trip around some ancient remnants and the sharing of the enthusiasm of the archaeologists themselves could be enhanced by a building that itself provides a wide variety of atmospheres and a myriad of directions and angles from which one comes upon a piece of history.

We felt strongly that the museum should allow some of its collection to trickle out from the chambers themselves. And we were very much inspired by the existing cloister. Here was a clue: perhaps the new building might be an extended series of cloisters, a series of racks within which the exhibits would be held and lit. The cloisters and racks would intermix. The visit to the museum would be a theatrical experience. A series of surprises. This seemed to work well with the need to homogenise the new chambers and the old: a roughly 50-50 ratio.

The building therefore consists of a path. You notice it from the outside, wrapping itself around the line of the display, 'gage', or 'mesh'. It starts to climb and enters the building. The new chambers sit upon a series of piers that create some of the new cloistering. Organisationally, the strong line of the cage is a regulating influence. Elsewhere in the building an analogous series of 'shop window' elements create, in negative, a further cage. Around these winds the path; it climbs, levels and then continues, snake-like, and eventually descends out of the building into the cloistered space.

The German word *blick* is key, for the 'glimpse' is an essential corollary to the full-frontal confrontation with an exhibited space. From the tradition of (particularly English) Gothic churches, we contrived to suggest and diffuse space by the intermission of the cage – a screen in the manner of certain choir screens. Light is coming from a high level, and often obliquely, again very much in the manner of a clerestory, or passed on to a tympanum.

All around the building there are points where one can glimpse through to the exhibits: from the Museum plaza at the west end are 'reverse-bay' windows that allow a special glimpse. Throughout the areas surrounding the building there are cage elements that protrude and carry pieces of the collection within; we wanted the museum to tantalise the passer-by as well as the seeker of knowledge. We wanted the spaces to be open and available to all, without destroying the magic of an unfolding interior.

It is fairly obvious that the project lies within our own work as a reinvestigation of two elements: the winding path and the mesh. The Trondheim library contains a winding path from which the building gradually opens up as a 'Gothic' space. The DOM office building also contains a winding path, which rises upwards within a central arcade/arboretum. (Incidentally, the Karmeliter and the DOM were being worked on simultaneously, both having a competition hand-in date of September 15). In the Karmeliter, there is the necessity to hug the walls of the old building very closely and the path does become a display place from time to time. But a generosity of scale is created by the relative 'heroism' of the total path. We were concerned to avoid the fussiness that often comes of a sensitive rehabilitation and addition game. Perhaps we offended the Frankfurters in the end, for we learn that some felt that we had in effect 'raped' the old church. The use of the 'mesh', 'cage', 'rack', 'screen', 'cloister' is rather different from that in other recent work such as the Linz pavilion and the Shadow House. In the latter, the mesh notion is allied, at least conceptually, with the notion of endless space and total diffusion, whilst in the Karmeliter the space is limited and, in addition, another demand is being made upon the cage element; it is, at lowest, a simple display device. It has another extreme role, however, analogous to that of the path itself, as a dominant regulator of the new with the old building. The east-west line of the rack can be seen as a kind of kebab stick upon which a series of otherwise disparate parts are (juicily?) strung. This leads to a couple of central notions in this building: the mimicry of the new strip on the southern side of the complex 'x' of the old strip (the nave/choir) on the northern side and secondly, the contrapuntal game that is always being played by the path *vis-à-vis* the rack line and later *vis-à-vis* the substance of the old building itself.

It may be significant that we had been looking closely at the work of Gunnar Asplund, and at Sigurd Lewerentz's Stockholm chapel (before finding a suitable excuse to take our students to see them). There are qualities of space and light understood and developed by the Swedish modern romantics that have until very recently been ignored. At the same time, Christine's interest in the work of Schreiter, Clarke and the transmitted light qualities of certain cathedrals could be overlaid. So in the design of plan and section, we pondered much longer than usual the precise placement of a path as it passed through an old opening, or made an angle of maybe only two and half degrees with its neighbouring parts.

The total image of the southern flank, the part that is at least 65 per cent a new building is deliberately dynamic. We became fascinated by the potential of a 1:20 incline to counteract the normal horizontals of the rack and the ground line. The administration block, containing laboratories and a lecture theatre, started to take off on its own and contains a continuous ramp corridor that winds around the rack-shaft. The lecture hall/library apse counterbalances that of the end of the Antiquities hall. The windows of the new parts of the building also continue a diatribe between the inclined angle and the horizontal and here we were making a slight (if obscure) reference to the tradition of Gothic window tracery in compounding oblique lines. At any rate, the development of the window openings is deliberately a progression from south to north, so that direct sunlight is avoided onto exhibits and very definite crescendo conditions are made with the window massing.

In many ways the design was a deliberate avoidance of the typical new German architecture with which we have become very familiar since we have been teaching in Germany, listening to local architectural gossip and becoming as well acquainted with *Bauwelt* as with *Building Design*. We get very bored by the typical gridded, slightly heavy 'sub-Ungers' schemes (I'm sure Ungers does too!) There always seems to be a cracked matrix, a patch of trees in serried ranks (little balls on the model) and a heavy portico-element.

The romantic influence, the waywardness of the lines, but the relative viciousness of the kebab-line apparently did not attract many jurors. Maybe we were lucky to even make Sixth Place? Yet there is another building in this one. For ourselves, the line from the Via Appia House, through Trondheim, DOM and the Karmeliter is suggesting a clear and manipulable series of strategies and parts. Even the Shadow House – a very different expressionistic image – follows the same general direction as the first but in a wayward manner. A series of spaces diffused by meshes and then revealed as one passes along the wayward path. When do we get to build one?

Architectural Association Quarterly, 1981

'TOWARDS ARCADIA'
Inventiveness as Design Culture

There is a cussed element of human psychology that is preserved throughout life by some people, and even reinforced self-consciously by a few. A certain egocentricity leads them to become dictators, original philosophic thinkers, or inventors. Inventors use the existing culture and its methods and technologies as a springboard for their own train of thought and if they grow up in a country where individualism is admired and eccentricity tolerated they are lucky. The English or North Americans refer to this type as the 'boffin'.

The simple boffin is content to create tangible objects that solve problems: machines, devices that save time, improvements to existing machines. But in the Anglo-Saxon world there is a related species, who sees his inventions or his thoughts as components of a different world. There is no dividing line between speculative inventors and dreamers. To complete the background we must add another type of permitted eccentric: the collector. In countries that are puritan and yet promote the individual, there is honour in privacy and in the pursuit of the very particular. There is no limit to the range of things that might be collected, from old cinema organs down to matchboxes. The atmosphere recalled by these things is as important as the comprehensive nature of the collection, so it is less necessary that the organ is played than that it conjures up the heyday of the Odeons as local palaces, as stylistically glamourous, as shrines to Mary Pickford and Douglas Fairbanks. Similarly, the matchbox no longer contains matches but reminds one of that very particular smell of an almost-forgotten brand of cigarette. Elsewhere we are discussing as environments some places that are really collections. The eccentric front garden, things made in miniature, or topiary are collections of objects that are separated by size or context or material from their sources, yet they comment on those sources either by making fun of them, or perhaps by expressing a wish to live in a more special world. So the imagination can, under special circumstances, be brought into tangible form, even if the Arcadia is the size of a window ledge.

In American life there has been a tradition of individual achievement and the staking-out of one's territory still underlies political and economic attitudes. It also supports the conscious escape of certain individuals from the East Coast (which they view as almost European in the 'establishedness' of its culture), or from other city belts. In architecture this can be sensed in the work of Bruce Goff, Paulo Soleri, the Drop City or the houseboats at Sausolito. It is a far cry from the 1970s school of New York which immediately communicated with Europeans because the games played by its architecture were consciously aware of European tradition. Even the consciously incorporated 'small town' aesthetic of Venturi and Rauch, or Moore and Turnbull was posed and urbane and conscious of the Ecole des Beaux-Arts. Goff and Soleri had traceable academic origins and were at some time in Frank Lloyd Wright's studio, but their work was inexorably linked with the 'West', the psychology of the commune, the individualist, the trekker, memories of the pueblos, and with Mexico as its aesthetic and spiritual model rather than Rome. Bruce Goff wove spider-like webs for his clients, and seemed in his houses to have retained that spooky but boyish spirit of the tree-house. Paulo Soleri has managed to convince others (mostly students) of the possibility of realising a dream city in the desert, so Arcosanti takes form as a giant bucket-and-spade enterprise for those who want 'out' from the campuses but also want to share an ideal.

There is a simplicity in this architecture of the outback, and an eccentricity of its form that immediately appeals to the idealist. Yet it is very often irritatingly naive, and given to form for form's sake, whereas the Easterners and Europeans develop architectural ideas by way of internal debate between certain elites (some of which are international) and references to selected pieces of history and selected seminal buildings. The saddest paradox of the last 20 years has been that both extreme groups, the outback expressionists and the urban literati, have made few new statements about social planning, the nature of buildings as amenities, or ways in which settlements can evolve.

It is essential to recognise the differences of scale and spirit between England and the United States. The collector of special junk in a London suburb and the college drop-out proclaiming an alternative community way up in the Rockies are not only different in habits and appearance. The scale of their escape affects the degree of abstraction, or turning aside from the world. It affects their absorption of mainstream cultures as well – though they might hate to admit it. Along with a self-consciousness about its decline, the English population has become obsessed with 'past times'. Nostalgia, encouraged by the Prince of Wales, is an intense national indulgence, occupying an immense proportion of television time and subject matter for popular novels. It infiltrates fashion in clothes and graphic design. More seriously, it is now a respectable retreat for architecture and many local authorities have returned to what is erroneously termed 'vernacular' as the stylisation of low-rise, 'cottagey' buildings. Again, as with much American work, they are quite mainstream and flaccid in their organisation and provision of real amenities. So this too is part of the international culture of stagnation, despite local tastes. Such architectural vernacularism lacks the real involvement of the 19th-century Romantic Movement, and there is little vision of an alternative world, forwards or backwards, to reinforce the reactionary state of the objects themselves. So we avoid the possibility of a scene of medieval dress and habits performed within a medieval dwelling, or Victorian manners, parlours or bigotry performed within apparently Victorian roofs. But we have something worse: a laissez-faire environment. It engenders short bursts of passing interest in periods of the recent past (as further nostalgia), and these come into fashion at increasingly rapid intervals. So it is that revivalist aesthetics have finally caught up with their own tail. What has been exploded is the force between historical necessity and the form of the object. Perhaps the mainstream culture is itself an escape, so where can we escape from that?

American escape psychology has not yet reached such a frightening stage, since there is basically more room in which to physically hide. On the other hand, there is also more suspicion of the eccentric. The hobo, the dweller in Arcosanti, and the freak, are seen as portents of the destruction of the hitherto optimistic, and essentially forward thrust of American society, so they are particularly unnerving now, when this thrust can be seen to weaken. There are few equivalents in the American Establishment of the British 'professional eccentric', who can receive a knighthood when his eccentricity has become loveable and the originality of his theories has been watered down; a subtle process whereby the dynamic of such people is watched and diluted into the mainstream.

The 20th century has therefore reached a difficult point for the tactile visionary, especially if his vision has societal implications. He can either present it as apparently orthodox, which is quite the reverse of the Modern Movement, where sometimes orthodox thinking had to present itself as apparently revolutionary. Or he can accept that overt alternatives may well remain as academic hypotheses (or drawn visions), for which the international architectural establishment and historicists have a moderate taste. Alternatively, he can head for the hills (in the case of America), a university institute (in the case of Europe), or his back garden (in the case of England), and make a microcosmic attempt at physical realisation.

Somewhere, in the inevitable cycle, vision must return to urban architecture, and the realisation that alternative lifestyles are possible, and even cheap and enjoyable.

In the Europe of the 19th century, the relationship of the inventor to the demands of a fast expanding economy resulted in the successful manoeuvring of boats up onto viaducts that carried canals, the drilling of longer and longer tunnels, the rack-and-pinion defying gravity at the most unassuming corners of bourgeois watering-places. And there were those devices for enabling genteel (but incontinent or lazy) people to carry out bodily functions with the least amount of travelling. In a sense, the commode is the ultimate Arcadian object; a world of ultimate comfort, convenience and sedentary pleasure, styled to look acceptable on any occasion.

Was the electric kitchen a direct successor? In some ways the excitement of the idea, which historically paralleled the model 'T' Ford and the notion of popular travel, could be described as a basic aesthetic breakthrough. Electric power and heat reduced the quantity of mechanical objects – pipes, valves and flues to a minimum, and thereby allied itself to the aesthetic of purist art. It is a dynamic force, electricity. We can call this a 'colonisation' of normal life by a realised ideal. An Arcadian colony that was understandable to the average housewife. In the 1930s there was still sufficient initiative in the Modern Movement of architecture for the

Electric Kitchen to be a natural ally to the transparency of glass, the free plan and the plastic structure.

There has been less success in late 20th-century Arcadian colonisation, even though the computer, magnetic tape and the microchip can fundamentally effect the systems that determine our lives. We can literally be tried in court, paid, employed or not employed, be killed by faulty navigation or poisoned by incorrect analysis as a result of these inventions. This is perhaps the most intense effect that artefactual colonisation has ever had, but its apparent physical presence is minimal. This can best be seen in the office, where the actual power of these devices is immense, but the apparently radical changes in the office environment are few. The Burolandschaft technique of scattering furniture, spreading clumps of vegetation amongst the desks and replacing rectilinear corridors with clumps of workplaces on an open office floor, are all picturesque devices that are almost Victorian in their symbolism and dependence on decoration. As they make a sweet attempt to alleviate the reality of the big organisation, the systems of real control and the chain of command herald the final triumph of the boffins. Elsewhere there have been modest excitements because architecture, using the current technologies, can explode the tightness of institutions and the inflexibility of buildings.

A whole generation of 'mechanised shed' buildings has been designed. The approach has been applied to hospitals and factories and even, possibly, housing. Yet the dream has not been fully realised. For in the 1970s a combined series of reactions – from wasteful high technology, to free-form events and de-institutionalism – pushed these buildings into the background and we returned to traditional types of organisation and traditional techniques of building. Only in industry has the software-inspired building continued to develop. So it can be seen that the dreams of inventors and the dreams of architects who might be inspired by inventors are filtered by those in power, or by the institutions, and there is still no proof that the man in the street might not like them.

Another problem exists when inventions or buildings cannot easily be recognised for what they are. This may be to do with scale, or simply with familiarity. It becomes very difficult when the components are microscopically small. A room, whether made of concrete or paper, is a comprehensible space. A cooker is a cooker, all the way through from the camp fire to the electric

frying-pan. The microchip however, is so small that it becomes more of a conceptual object than a physical object. So 'software' as a word is particularly apt to describe the family of systems, procedures, intangibly rapid instructions and mathematical gymnastics that exist as electrical impulses. The tape deck and the desk-top computer keyboard are poor monuments to the idea. You can too easily confuse the computer, the typewriter or the electric piano, and we are still too close to the world of the roll-top desk, the study or the church organ. So parallel to the collective cynicism that surrounds the issue of the truth of the object there is a frightening explosion of the recognition of the object. There is a real difficulty of communication between the instigative dreamers and the ordinary untutored, dreamers of dreams. Science fiction has repeatedly to invoke the visions and symbols of traditional tales in order to hold the reader's imagination. A much more difficult task for those who design scientific fact.

Reyner Banham has been virtually the only serious architectural critic to dwell upon these problems. He has featured burger-bars, watches, cartoon characters, fascias on shops, calculators and motorbikes out of the category of dismissible ephemera, and has worried away at the questions they posed to architects, engineers, politicians and sociologists. Not only has he asked what is their role and their style, but what fundamentals of our culture they challenge:

Far more than whatever technologies of back-projection and travelling mattes may go into these (*Thunderbirds*) scenes, it is a study of real vehicles in motion that pays off . . . (it) gets close enough to produce in-joke situations: there was that Ferrari-eating model 'T' Ford (itself an in-joke for the hot-rod crush) for instance. In the coming-at-you shots its front wheels fluttered and its axle tramped as to the vintage manner born, as an almost exact visual carbon of a sequence with an ancient Alfa Romeo in a Shell instructional film . . . now if I was a sort of cultural Vance Packard, I could make a small fortune . . . if I pursued . . . Lady P's (a puppet) relationship with her man Parker because this marginally Chatterly figure also subsumes elements of Jeeves, Raffles, Sam Weller, Jack Benney's Rochester and Willie Garvin as well . . . my personal interest in *Thunderbirds* is as an equipment drama. At this level its bird life can function as an epitome of its ultimate superiority.[1]

Banham was always keen to relate the hot images and the laughable quirks of popular culture, old tricks and known stories. So even the dumbest main street in middle America can be seen to have some comment to make on, say, the neo-Classic revival, however mixed-up. Or the Classic revival upon the dumb street.

Robert and Denise Venturi tried to get under this as well. In a much more pedantic way, their study *Learning From Las Vegas*, examined all the tat and the apparent inconsequentiality of the objects along the strip and brought our attention to the actual sophistication and urbanity of it. So there has begun a state almost bordering on nostalgia, or conscious escapism towards the American strip. The architecture is as much the accumulation of the gadgetry as it is the accumulation of facades. So the electricity poles, the air conditioners, the garages, the reassuring electric sign, the beckoning burger sign or the sign for gas – they are the 20th-century parallel to the quiet close of cottages, with reassuring smoke coming up from the chimneys. At this moment it is the role of intellectuals to wax enthusiastic, but so it was in the early 19th century, before the suburb developers could realise that reconstructed Arcadias might be profitable.

Optimistically then, this explosion that *image* and *device* have undergone, a painful separation, could lead to some Arcadian colonisations. A scary one is the possible infiltration of the home into the workplace. Or the corollary – not necessarily frightening – of the institutionally-based activity infiltrating the home. Could there be a cosy, homely atmosphere in parts of a factory? Especially now, when so much of the messier element is automised and the control point does not need to look like a workbench. At the other end, the idea of receiving lectures and information at home was the basis of the establishment of the Open University (originally to be called, more evocatively, the 'University of the Air'). The model in operation has rapidly become less and less 'open' and less and less discernable from older models of the academic institution. In the 1960s there were many dreamers of the concept of a whole nation able to indulge in learning by switching on a television set, whilst still lying in bed, and discussing ideas with real tutors by videophone, or with robot tutors somewhere at the end of a wire. The whole country became a quiet, 'soft' academe and it was one of the most Arcadian notions of our time.

Leisure and its potential have been repeatedly held forth as the next major goal of civilisation: an Arcadia that consists of opportunity for self-expression, or, more cynically, a third part of organised existence to add to work and travelling and it seems inevitable that we must satisfy the tremendous expectancy of those who live in developed and industrialised countries. In Japan, this is most pertinent. Society there has been dominated by paternalism, so that your lifestyle, your choice of wife, your pension, your working operation, your blue shirt or white shirt (but rarely a *green* shirt) have traditionally been ordained by the Family or the Company. But the possibility of leisure time exists; leisure activity, a piece of space in which to escape that (interchangeable) Family and Company, a faster breaking of the shackles than the temporary Arcadia offered by the love-hotel or the television soap-opera, which are merely overlays upon the traditional life. The mad enthusiastic acquisition of consumer products is an expression of this same desire for escape; yet it remains a mere cosmetic that is applied to a static social pattern. So the increase in free time will at some point reach a magical dimension at which a chasm of life will be fully opened up, the rituals of traditional family life will be exploded and the offerings of the company will be seen in perspective. Such an emancipation seems at least as significant as that of industrialisation itself.

In Europe, we already have the experience of 'extracted time'. The two-week or three-week Spanish holiday is perhaps more explosive than the ownership of the family car, for the latter served only to elasticate existing habits. In its early stages the foreign holiday had to be presented with the trappings of familiarity, so the fish-and-chip dinner – an essential part of the old Blackpool holiday – needed to be there on the Costa Brava. But the feedback into daily life has commenced. Eating can be considered as a colonisation process, and every American, English, German or Dutch small town has a Mediterranean restaurant of some kind, if not several. The taste for oily, sharp flavours has infiltrated the world of potatoes, sausages and beer and memories of those three weeks in the sun are conjured up by pasta and guitar music. At the next stage, wrought iron railings appear in the backyard and the stranglehold of climate and custom is attacked. We look forward, with our travel brochures, to the second holiday at Easter and, with more leisure still, to a few more days in the autumn.

We are presented with a challenge: the Arcadia of the future may not be that of an alternative sheltered valley, but the fruits of invention, of software programmes and cultural liberalism and the simultaneous existence of a parallel world rather than an alternative. At the present stage, the taste for the exotic is once again part of the game, just as it was for the privileged classes in the 18th and 19th centuries, so we are attracted to both the Moorish holiday, and the Moorish window decoration, the Greek ruin and Classical wallpaper. Despite the totally different context and dynamic, and the fact that the reproduction or reminder back home is a poor thing by comparison with its inspiration, we love to indulge in these associations, just as did the rich bourgeoisie with their bits of chinoiserie in those old Berlin villas. The next generation of boffins may need to recognise this need, as perhaps they have already in the cinema.

The inventors can already sense that their strength lies in infiltrating the movements by which we are all, slowly, being emancipated. At the same time, however, we become punch drunk. There is a noticeable diminution of public excitement as each invention is announced. We have come to *expect* innovation. We are dependent upon it for our survival. So the real significance of the 'microchip revolution' has to be elaborately explained, and underlined in order to attract our attention. It is *intangible as hardware*. It is almost intangible as an idea, because it cannot easily be compared with any of our traditional artefacts. This says something for the tradition of the visual – and the strength of this tradition, as distinct from the tradition of the aesthetic.

In some ways too, the 20th century has retained the need for humanism in the face of the abstract or the superhuman. Trees, animals, gates, hedges, boats, cars and even most aeroplanes have a relationship with our human size and human habits, so it doesn't matter that the list includes old, friendly objects and newer, mechanised objects. At least we use them and know them and relate to them, they are touchable and visible. The next generation of inventions is far more difficult to relate to, and some cultural language will need to develop to make the minute and the unseen as loveable.

The 20th century has been a time of physical action: wars, films, machines, transportation; and an opportunity for exciting us is offered by providing action: even distilled or false. Here it is worth relating the attempts by visual artists to implode some activity into art pieces. In no way can Tinguely's creations match the workings of a newspaper print room, or even a small car. The mechanistic artist can only comment on the sidelines of real dynamics, as an ironic cartoonist watching the trajectory of the machine developing onwards to its inbuilt destruction: the vortex, by which it seems that the scale of motivational power is becoming involved, gets smaller and smaller and conceptually it almost becomes anti-matter. But there is a fundamental difference between creative boffins and creative artists. If the former are more powerful in simple terms of the effect of their work upon our survival, the latter have always been able to offer vision as well as speculation; a vision that has often combined the unlike and offered a deliberate distortion of familiar objects.

The basis of so much art has been in the symbolic power of chosen images. Distortion then comes in many ways: exaggeration, irony, deformation, the degree of intellectualisation. Indulgence in this distortion, not only, as in the case of Braque or Picasso, in the choice of the degree of abstraction as against figuration, but the playing out of the role of ultimate collagist. For, like the player of a war game or an alchemist, the artist can mix and scramble unlike elements of totally different dimension, value, culture, origin. He can choose to invert and select conventional sets of association, or hierarchies, or proportions. Hence our continued fascination with the Surrealists, long after the cycle of fashion should have waned for them. They attract many non-visual people by their absurd propositions, and by their frequent science-fiction quality.

It is a paradox then, that the artist who has been the fountainhead of conceptual art, and therefore of the reaction of artists themselves away from easy visual communicability, has produced the most challenging art piece of all, still containing amazing piquancy in its choice of component images, and attempting a synthesis of ideas about time, space, programme and cultural symbolism. Marcel Duchamp's *The Bride Stripped Bare by her Bachelors, Even* (The *Large Glass*) is the product of several simultaneous preoccupations. In Richard Hamilton's words[2] it is: 'born of Duchamp's perversity. It springs from the intensity of his will to seek only within himself the rules of a game of his own devising . . . his interest in chronophotographic representation of movement . . . a mechanomorphic object in a limitless, one-dimensional space . . .' There are combinations of dimension, elevations and perspectives and references to mathematics. 'Einstein's theory of relativity was just then (1915-23) being discussed at a superficial level in the popular press, and Duchamp gave an ironic twirl to the notion of the standard meter being modified by

movement through time and space'.

Perverse and original techniques are used by the artist, not only to free his work from the familiar connotations of paint and texture and blandness of representation, but the intensity and *accuracy* of the programme is that of the inventor or scientist. In the drawing process, chance and games theory are involved and Hamilton speculates: 'If the Large Glass is a representation of a three-dimensionalised world on a two-dimensional surface, then could a three-dimensional representation be a conventional projection of a four-dimensional world?' Later conceptual artists, though exploding the dominance of imagery upon art, return to much narrower territories. In a sense, it is left to architects to deal with the synthesising of time, atmosphere and relationships.

If individual visionaries among the boffins or artists have been able to pose their private Arcadias, the question remains whether the population at large can learn from the history of art or the history of invention. It is within the grasp of the man in the street to go beyond his powers and distort the limitations of action, to *really* use time (whether as an extension of the conventional idea of 'recreation', or more originally) and gear themselves to a world of distorted and unexpected mixtures of experience. Thus science fiction must be read as a preliminary introduction to reality, rather than as an escape from it. The colonisation of the moon, and its tedious limitation to the status of a rather inconvenient laboratory, has disappointed us because it failed to offer a site for the living out of Edwardian or early-Futurist dreams. So the moon-city of the Adventure Comics is an obsolete model. However, to use this as an excuse to retreat back to the cosy suburbs and Grandma's ethics is too simple. To grapple with the new dynamics is more frightening, and may have no pre-existent imagery, but we can use the offerings of the new teaching systems in schools, the ultimate in deaf-aids, life-support pills, the possible arcadia of free-time and the ultimately discoverable *other nice planet* as markers.

How serious was Heath Robinson – that inventor of domestic quaintness and a world where British whimsey was able to anticipate the labour-saving ideology of the mid-20th century? Or the more indulgent Roland Emmett of the 1950s? Could Simon Rodilla have designed a whole city, given time and a whole team of welders and tilers? It is comfortable to relegate them to the corners of the invented world, but they had the power to communicate, perhaps through the innate

simplicity of their propositions which underlay their apparent complexity of line. Heath Robinson used the role of the cartoonist, perhaps because he was part of a bourgeois world that enjoyed a daft idea with a glass of port, or that tolerated the expression of strong feeling provided it was satirised. We have only to look at the viciousness of political statements and criticism in the 19th-century newspaper cartoons to speculate that the preposterousness of Heath Robinson's inventions could be easily digested. Two generations later, Emmett used the same medium; his work became the darling of the Establishment and his mock vehicles and machines were constructed as exhibits in national fairs. Rodilla, on the other hand, could only build his towers in a dusty and under-privileged part of Los Angeles. It is not enough to regard him as a sweet old chap, and his buildings as pretty toys. The attempts by the City to remove them were beaten by the innate strength of the fabric. Now, of course, they are revered and frequently appear in serious books on architecture. Yet they are still regarded as a one-off event, and rarely examined as a very useful model of the relation of structural fabric to decorative art, or as a pointer to the way in which rooms might be organised in space, or vertical buildings might be more acceptable if less bland and less solid.

The ultimate inventor of our period is Richard Buckminster Fuller, and his one man's output is itself the proof of optimism. The objects are innovative, the structures are understandable and cheap. The contextual offerings are at once exciting and directly related to the imagery of the objects. So excited does he become with his inventions, that they lead to greater and greater statements of universality. The story of his life is that of a continuing search for comprehensiveness which leaves behind the limits of designed objects as merely sufficient unto themselves and their function. So the titles of the projects have a heroic ring: the 'World Town Plan' (1927), the 'World Energy Map' (1940), the 'Geospace' dome (1961). Some demand the total invention of a nomenclature and terms of reference, so original are both their concepts and their hardware: the 'Dymaxion' house (1927), the 'Dymaxion' bathroom (1937), Energetic and 'Synergetic' geometry (from about 1940). Others are in a constant dialogue with concepts of nature: the 'Mini-Earth' sphere (1952) and the 'Seed-Pod' structures (1950s). In 1962 he himself wrote:

My experience is now world-around . . .
I have been operating on the philo-

sophic premise that all thoughts and experiences can be translated much further than just into words and abstract thought patterns. I saw that they can be translated into patterns which may be realised in various physical projections – by which we can alter the physical environment itself and thereby induce other men to subconsciously alter their ecological patterning . . . none of the other species have altered their ecological patterning . . . in the last half century man has graduated from a local 12-mile radius daily domain into a world around multi-thousand mile radius daily domain . . . as a consequence of his ability to alter his own ecological patterning . . . I am convinced that humanity is characterised by extraordinary love of its new life to such an extent that the new life is continually at greater disadvantage than it would be if abandoned in the wilderness by its parents . . . up to the time I was nine years old, the idea that man could fly was preposterous . . . I have lived deeply into a time when flying is no longer impossible, but nonetheless a period in which the supremely ruling social conventions and economic dogma have continued to presuppose a nonflying man ecology.[3]

The vision of the existent world that can be extended to another state of comprehension is reinforced by the musician/conceptualist, John Cage. As Duchamp started from the position of visual artist and then proceeded audaciously to strip away the limitations of the visual tradition, replacing them by analysis as well as by the extension of his craft; and as Fuller started as an engineer, and then enthusiastically layered and layered-in segments of an overview, so Cage departs from the reproductive and purely tonal language of music to explore time and space as well as sonic impact. He observes that: 'Art's obscured the difference between art and life. Now let life obscure the difference between life and art. Fuller's life is art: comprehensive design science, inventory of world resources (if enough mined copper exists, re-use it, don't mine more: same with ideas). World needs arranging. It'll be like living in a painting by Jasper Johns: Stars and Stripes'll be utilities, our daily lives the brushstrokes.'[4]

A reintegration is therefore needed between the sciences and the other territories that have become separated by institutions and cultures. These artist-strategists are rare, and considered to be eccentric. There are also those people around the fringes of architecture who have been inspired by selected futurology and speculate on what might happen if our present pursuits of television or travelling and our dependence upon stimuli of one kind or another are taken to the point of doom or inertia, or the much greater use of our planet and our brains. At the moment, such conversations are out of fashion, but perhaps only temporarily. Next time round they will need inventors, artists and architects of *at least* the imagination of the 18th-century gardeners and carpenters.

Notes
1 Reyner Banham, 'The Gadget People', *New Society*, 24 March 1966.
2 *Marcel Duchamp*, ed Richard Hamilton, Museum of Modern Art, New York, 1973.
3 Richard Buckminster Fuller, *Education Automation*, Carbondale, 1962.
4 John Cage, *A Year From Monday* and the *Aspen Papers*.

Peter Cook, 1983

AN ARCHIGRAM LEGACY

The strength of the Archigram Group was undoubtedly the fact that no two members were very similar. Not only did we all study at different colleges, but our ages spanned 11 years and our accents almost parody the regionalism of even such a small country as the UK. Left to our own devices, we would almost certainly split off in the evenings into several different corners, though we all would read rather more magazines than is generally thought to be culturally respectable. If not magazines, then manifestos, if not manifestos, then reports of long-lost manifestos.

In other words, there was indeed a self-conscious awareness amongst us that the history of the 20th-century architecture was not only a history of heroic stances, heroic acts and heroic pronouncements, but a history of absurd geometries, audacious exhibits and the overlaying of a series of cut-and-thrust phenomena. Each of us had arrived (without initial collusion) at the conclusion that good architecture (and that meant 'interesting' architecture – which probably meant 'naughty' architecture) had always been resisted by the broad swathe of the general population. After we had finally all met, we started to share some secrets with each other and started to grumble. This attitude hardened and focused upon an assumed 'enemy'. Had not Gropius, Le Corbusier and the Smithsons had conspicuous enemies? They were always there . . . and the *them* became formalised as implying timid, reactionary, obstructive or even just disinterested other architects. 'This'll upset *them*' was the rallying cry as one swung another naughty airship or contentious squiggle onto the axonometric.

Modernism went without saying. We regarded ourselves as automatically '*after* Modern' as we were making things that were outside the Modernist vocabulary. But we admired the pluck of the old Modern. It had balls. Thinking of my own introduction to architecture, I remember that an established family mythology had been created. My father was an army officer who, having had a very active 1914-18 war, was determined to stay out of the mud in the war of 1939-45. Without any knowledge of surveying or architecture he became the Colonel in charge of 'quartering' for a large chunk of the Midlands. This involved motoring out to large

Italianate mansions, taking an infantryman's eye to them, and then pronouncing them useful to 'tanks' or 'two platoons of US paratroops', or whatever. His four-year-old son found it great fun. I managed to continue on these trips until the age of nine by assiduous avoidance of 'games' afternoons. I have never therefore been much good at cricket but am able to site a one-battalion camp by fingering the wind, looking for the drainage stream and assessing the width of the farm gate – the less fancy influence upon one's architectural instincts than the 'Italianness' of the villas, but the more memorable. From the age of eight I wanted to be a Modern architect. Not an architect. A *Modern* architect. In the public library I bypassed the books about castles and palaces and cathedrals (I'd read those anyway and had lived in at least three medieval cathedral cities . . . that was no fun) but these whitewalled things . . . foreign names . . . bombastic ideas . . . that was the thing!

David Greene and Warren Chalk had wanted to be painters, perhaps that is why, out of all of us, they have always had the greatest self-doubt, reluctance to draw to order, sense of both the irony and the poetry of things. The intensity of what they have drawn is therefore the sweeter and probably more significant.

Mike Webb is the genius, the *absolute* original of the bunch. You can almost never trace where he could have got his ideas from. The rest of us have always chatted about it, so that an intelligent listener could probably predict the next moves and certainly trace the observed images. I am told that his early work at the Regent Street Polytechnic was inspired by Le Corbusier, but by 1958, when his Furniture Factory was designed, the *direct* Webb architecture – emanating from two or three simply stated ideas – had emerged. The ideas, incidentally, were about 'racks', 'swelling to enclose' and 'ferro-cemento' (the last the technical means to achieve the first two). His path was best known to himself, although he has never been so private as to refuse to say what he has been trying to do. However the puzzle (or is it?) is that his explanation always sounds so simple.

Dennis Crompton is the least explained member, partly because he has hardly more

than three identifiable drawings to his name. Yet anyone who has observed Archigram in action will know that he often holds the key to the problem. He has spent years on the floor of the exhibition hall, or the bench of the printers, or at the end of the blowpipe, or explaining to the rest of us what it is that we are really trying to do, and how we might do it more easily. Sometimes he has been explained away as our technologist, but the English word 'boffin' is best.

So it was that Ron Herron and myself, with our different backgrounds and directions – he having built several schools and I merely a provincial enthusiast via the arrogant finishing school of the AA – were the two who would just keep drawing. We would buy books (of more drawings) and listen, occasionally, to the criticism of the others who had more doubts, but not for long enough to slow us down . . . drawing.

Teaching was inevitable; as inevitable as those other pieces of the avant-garde apparatus that we had observed in books and magazines and gossip: exhibitions, pamphlets, rhetoric, gatherings, competitions. None of us could have forecast how great a part in our lives it would play . . . to both good and bad effect. Its generativeness must surely come from the fact that most of it has been made at the Architectural Association, surely the only English institution that is designed for the absorption of the contentious, the outrageous or the aesthetically inclined. This absorption means that quite a large measure of your energy is consumed by students who are pushy, self-possessed and probably as talented as you are. They are going to make damned sure that your creative energy deals with *their* ideas or paranoias first, before letting you take up some space interesting them or their friends with *your* ideas or paranoias. So it is a toughening-up condition. It results in the discovery that the most sycophantic, most imitative students recede into the memory the second day that you know them and that the *real* architectural conversations are with the adversaries, the mystics, the eccentrics and even the unmodern.

Around teaching there lurks always the 'ongoing conversation'. Especially in England, where it has been said that the 'architectural conversations are the best in the world and the ongoing buildings are the worst'. It stems from the national assumption that even the least important person must be heard, but even the most important person may not be listened to. It results in less compartmentalised 'grumbling' than in German architectural circles and less speech-making. We deliberately set up the printed *Archigram* sheet as a prompt to these conversations. Initially a *cri de coeur* from frustrated graduates, whose idealism did not seem to be represented in the buildings being built, the sheet soon developed into a talking shop about expendability. The coincidence that several contributors to issue No 2 (1962) chose this theme led to its becoming a virtual manifesto issue by No 3 (1963). Reyner Banham noticed us and championed our cause. Cedric Price emerged as a kind of 'witty cousin' figure, later to grow into the only consistently relevant ideas-person on the London scene with a conscience. None of us within the Group has his cleverness, nor the acerbity of his taste in architecture. However, best of all are his conversations. Even the dullest student project can become a magical *possibility* when washed by his mind and his enthusiasm.

There was a horrifying moment in 1968 or 69 when it looked as if the AA School, *Architectural Design* magazine and the Cedric Price office were all about to be closed down. Nothing to do with May 68, Modern/Post-Modern watersheds, philosophies; just money – mostly. Such is the fragility of the English scene. In retrospect, 1969 should have been fairly comfortable. But, it has remained the province of the *them* for all of that time. Pretty disinterested in all the things that might now be gathered together to form a positive Modernotech exhibit, the AA therefore provided a hot house in which Price could come (from the studied detachment of one street's distance) and deliver his latest observations on the socio-political relevance of beeswax (and heaven help anyone who left the room).

The healthiest thing that happened to Archigram was that it was not only teaching, but was forced to teach in a place where it was answered back, even mistrusted. The mistrustful eyes of one Nicholas Grimshaw (amongst my first ever group of students) became a little more friendly over the months. It was he who built (with Terry Farrell) the plug-in plastic bathroom tower in Bayswater. His persistence in confronting the Paddington Fire Officer 40 times was worth 100 paragraphs of supportive rhetoric. The members of Chrysalis huffed and puffed and

were all into tents and inflatables and things that might walk. Furthermore, they could not escape from us when they moved on as graduate students to Los Angeles, because Ron, Warren and I (it just happened) went there as well!

For me the Los Angeles break was incredibly important. As a seaside adolescent I had unselfconsciously absorbed the trick of the seaside town that could extend and retract – come alive and go almost dead – according to season and population (surely the origins of Plug-in City). LA was the seaside town to end all seaside towns. It was very London as well depending socially on that same way of mixing together eccentrics, but not making the same demands of protocol as New York or Paris, leaving one the option to 'disappear' or 'appear'. Most of all, though, it was optimistic and a natural collage of the unlike with the unlike. Instant City was first drawn right there. It brought Ron and I into daily contact with Arata Isozaki and a weird group of graduates from Graz. Out of Chrysalis (who later gravitated to the Rogers team on Beaubourg – which explains plenty) and Gurngross Kichter, Helmuth Schultz and even, perhaps, the intriguing yes/no, love/hate of Eric Moss and his friends for mechanisation, came the independent legacy of Archigram.

We might have been partly responsible for the free fall, why draw? Strategy-is-all period at the AA (though at its height, Ron and I kept drawing, probably rather like chain-smokers or gum-chewers we found it soothing). Yet out of this period came some of the best intellects with whom I have ever worked. In particular, Colin Fournier, who was more strategically influential on the Archigram 'Monte Carlo' building than anyone else. His rigorous French schooling made him the ideal sparring-partner – allowing me to play the English expressionist buffoon – each of us tantalising the other's position. I can reconstruct the parallel roles played by Warren Chalk and Ron Herron in their pre-Archigram period (in which they, along with Dennis Crompton and others would consistently win second prize in competitions but never first). The elastic-fingered Herron, would be bugged by Chalk's dour but precise attack on the weak point and Chalk tantalised by the optimism of that same elasticity. At a later period the role-playing has been exercised by Christine Hawley and myself, able (this time) to take on either role. She has the more precise mind and I am interested in strategies but we both take it in turns to play the fool, idea-wise or drawing-wise. It is best on days when we have

decided upon complementary roles – though often invigorating (and completely bewildering for our collaborators) when we both decide to out-daft each other.

In recent years the business of drawing has become central to the debate of architecture and, in addition, it has become a discussion-worthy adjunct to those other listed elements of the avant-garde debate (the manifestos etc) and has the inevitable advantage of offering the *experimental* condition. This is why one gets bored by those who use architectural drawing to serve up rigid offerings that are already available to the viewer in the street. Now Archigram is seen by some as a pioneer in its revival, yet I have tried to explain that we never stopped drawing, nor did we consciously accelerate when the rest started to draw as well. It has always been linked to ideas, that is all. The style of drawings is far more complex. Mike Webb draws incredibly slowly – an inch a day it is said. Sometimes an inch a week. His school drawings showed complete control of the hard pencil and pencil-like use of the crayon when needed. In style he is like a miniaturist with every leaf of a tree, every plate of a metal-covered form, every joint of a pipe in place. His diffusion of the building proposition from Sin Centre (ink drawn) through Cushicle (ink diagram) to Suitaloon (ink diagram) to 'Dreams Come True' demanded a further shift. After 'Dreams' he taught himself oil painting which took maybe two years. Still, however, with the concentration of the miniaturist.

Ron Herron is essentially a graphic communicator. It was surely his policy decision that led the older half of Archigram (Herron, Chalk, Crompton) to use big fat pens on all their competitions 'so that it would reproduce one inch high in the *Architects Journal*'. By comparison, the rest of us were weedy drawers, but we too picked up the fat pen technique for a while. David Greene could draw anything he wanted and it immediately had that painterly, atmospheric quality. Christine Hawley, too, has this ability. It has been my salvation that I have been constantly surrounded by those who could draw better than I, and so I could not let the side down. There is the alternative post-rationalisation of course, that if you sweat through the communication of an idea, the chances are that you have given it some thought. Since the advent of Cook and Hawley we have slowly shifted our graphic ground. Airbrush is used where sleekness or a certain manufactured softness is to be conveyed. Pencil crayons are infinitely controllable but can look 'dead'. Christine nearly always resorts to water: water-colour, water over airbrushing, water over crayon, since she fears the somewhat mechanical nature of so many architectural drawings. Recently we have started to use bas-reliefs to animate our drawings. Ironically, our own students draw quite differently from us, some of them with far better line. But we are fast. In Hamburg last September, Christine, Ron and I (with one student) were drawing at the rate of two metres (detailed stuff) a day! Like writing, it tries desperately to catch up with the rate of the idea/conversation when it goes well. In Hamburg it was like singing along to a catchy tune. I am always suspicious of drawings with large areas of hatching – the masturbation of the uninspired.

The most exciting aspect of recent years has been the sheer exploratory quality of the drawings of our friends and rivals. For instance, Peter Salter, who studied with Christine and myself as well as with Bernard Tschumi, is almost as slow as Webb and in many ways similar to him as an original fashioner and delver. His partner, Christopher Macdonald, on the other hand, comes from a (now lost) dreamy period at the AA when atmosphere and texture and spirit

were held more important than guts and skin (the props for David Greene and I). When mixed with Salter's technological quirks, it works. I can even remember when Peter Wilson was sloppy, but not for long; his 'Water House' is surely one of the most important architectural images of the 1970s . . . and it could only have been drawn. Similarly Zaha Hadid's flying and cutting graphics can only be described as supra-architectural. They extend the conversation beyond the point at which it can reasonably be expected to reach but not beyond the point at which it must be conjectured.

It is impossible to write a definitive list of pointers or markers in a short essay. One does however, constantly grumble about the fact that they (the critics, historians, career journalists, wise guys, etc) always get it wrong and miss out the good bits, so here is my list:

1   The Yellow 'Auto Environment' drawing of Mike Webb is probably the summary statement of Archigram philosophy: folding, electrics, trees, attenuation, the lot.

2   A brilliant scheme of the 1970s was the Trondheim Library by David Greene and Hans Hiegel (then his student). Since that

time David hasn't published his drawings and Hiegel has gone drearily Post-Modern.

3   The Cook-Hawley Trondheim Library is another special (even though I say it myself). We still eat ideas off that one, surreptitiously of course.

4   The jibe that Archigrammers are non-political fades in the light of Ron Herron's 'Sets fit for a Queen' . . . look at it, read it, think again. Recent photographs of Mr Herron spending the afternoon with Her Majesty notwithstanding (I was there and it was true).

5   Bernard Tschumi worked with me on one competition – an unsuccessful attempt for a Casino in Monte Carlo. From that point (1971 or so) I knew that he would be a really good building designer if given the chance. Last week in La Villette mud, he proved the point.

6   The Computer City should be wired into London by now. The Cushicle should be available in Harrods. The Shadow House should be sitting astride the Alps. The next scheme we do will be the really weird one though!

Peter Cook, February 1986

ARCHITECTURE IS ART

At no other time has it been easier to establish that architecture not only is art, but must be art. The present state of technology already makes it possible and economical to design any required building type to be the optimal response to user requirements. All that is necessary is for the computer to be intelligently briefed and efficiently programmed. Then the drawings and the building strategy can be prepared without any of the errors, waywardness or wilfulness of architects acting – as they do – with various fanaticisms, prejudices, bizarre rituals, funny habits as well as private jokes amongst themselves.

The old strategic argument that the difference between mere building and architecture was the availability of more expertise and content in the latter begins to be a questionable one. I for one am quite willing to believe that the whole history of architecture can be read as the assembly of avoidances of the issue (of shelter, defence, economy) as much as the exploitation of the issue. Architects are, you see, quite capable of having an amusing time with reality. Architecture is an enormous theatre of hocus-pocus with successive generations of visionaries or indulgers inventing sets of ritual and symbol to post-rationalise their games, and, if possible, to keep the droning questions about 'rightness', 'usefulness' and 'solidarity' off their backs.

And I am wholeheartedly in favour of the silliness. The computer only serves to reinforce the differences between 'rightness' and 'magic'. With all its prosaic inevitability it reminds you of the village know-all.

So far as one can tell, the existence of art has reminded even the most jaded of cynics or pessimists (if they have stopped to think) that there is significance in almost every play of light, conjunction of geometries, heap of dung, ripple of green into yellow, hint of a smile, cut of glass, and that the artist is extraordinarily lucky in being able to extend the normal boundaries of reality. This, by the way, has nothing to do with the chosen style or the chosen degree of reality or abstractness, since it can exist almost as soon as someone declares art to be present. Art is to do with the continuous battle that we have with the banality of reality. There is, in many corners of our society, a conspiracy towards

the denial of all this. In Norway they have a traditional philosophy (which fortunately they don't all subscribe to) called *junte-lov*, which means that 'he should not let his head appear above the wall' – basically implying that you should not do anything too special. What a terrible idea. Art seems to be the opposite of this . . . the search for specialness, the dabbling and wheedling that leads to the creation of a special circumstance out of apparently commonplace materials – even as restricted as small pieces of board and messy, sticky pigment in some cases.

How immensely suitable, then, is architecture as art. For it takes as an a priori the placement of the subject (victim-actor-gameplayer) in a place where all kinds of tricks may be played backwards and forwards between magic and reality, expected situation and surprise, function and theatre, even games of hide-and-seek or distortion, and, naturally, having recourse to the occasional use of the prosaic as a form of punctuation between all of these.

Some decades ago there was, of course, the lovable indulgence in the idea of functionalism. This could be allied to a timely idealism concerning public welfare and high socialism. We can, with hindsight, concern ourselves with the ironies of 'do-gooding' and the emancipation of the proletariat, along with what was often very dogmatic and insistent architecture. The fact that this architecture is, by the way, often to my own taste serves more to point out the irony than to ameliorate it – since the things that I and my friends enjoy about the white architecture are purely the art aspects: the cardboardness of the walls, the translucency of the glass strips, the acrobaticness of the structure. Art is quite a clever old game, using various wheezes of opportunism vis-à-vis the political situation, the boredom of monarchs, the boredom with the familiar (whether it be downtown, father's shoes or flat roofs that probably distinguishes 'cultured' Western Society from others).

By the way, I love all these cynicisms of the old Western city tradition. You sit in the coffee-house or pub (where Strindberg, Loos, Lutyens, Paganini used to sit?), and however outrageous – and, of course, immensely witty and original and deft – your own sketches or town plans or arpeggios are, their ghosts are sitting at another table

egging you on to be even more witty and at the same time reminding you of their own mystery. One might suggest, then, that the most despicable type of architecture is that which bores you. Broadly this is true – for if art is the fruit of imagination bursting out from the confines of banality then art-architecture must be that too.

As a proposition it needs a little amplification, however. There are those cultivated cases of architecture that so exactly tune their apparent banality as to seem to egg you on vampishly to search out the specialness within them. Sometimes there is a double-take, and they just turn out to be boring after all, but our arrogance rarely admits that we have been 'had'. Equally, there are those richly-scored pieces that are so insistent with tricks and symbols and things to look at that one cries out to get back on the bus. Interestingly, this can also apply to buildings that are organically fruity but where the architect (and perhaps his critic friend) have been so busy pointing out what a clever boy he has been, that the art – that is to say the magic – has been lost. The odd American architect (but I won't say who) has been particularly tiresome in this respect in recent years . . . I think it is something to do with the Americans' tremendous respect for culture, unlike us Europeans, who just wink at the old ghost in the corner and giggle at our own audacities.

There is a certain conflict of observable traditions in all of this, for in the Anglo-Saxon world in particular, the verbal culture has remained in the strongest position and a number of clever architects have cottoned on to the idea that the making of references is a good idea. These references are of course visual or pictorial, since it is architecture that we are talking about. Yet the nature of the reference seems often to be very much concerned with the cleverness of the allusion rather than the quality of the visual or pictorial element, and even less (if at all) with the effective condition that it gives to the actual place. In saying so I admit to a prejudice: I am more intrigued by 'things' and 'atmospheres' and 'sequences' than by dry reference. I am of course a product of the English picturesque tradition – and persuasion. This brings its own benefits and traps. The benefits are essentially concerned with romanticism and small-scale nuance. The traps are concerned with a certain crafty sweetness: I recommend you all to beware the English architect when he starts to hold forth about the process and the detail – having skated over the appalling lack of basic composition or dynamic in his building.

One English characteristic that I do find useful is however to be derived from our literary tradition – the narrative path that runs in a gently indirect way, casting occasional sidelong glances into character or vista and throwing half-light upon incidents along the way – but rarely reaching a definite conclusion. Part of the mode of life that shuns both political extremism or even definition as well as philosophical determinism. It often appears both indecipherable and irritating to those of the French or German intellectual tradition, yet in its inconsistent and indulgent way it is a marvellous basis for artistic speculation. To take a characteristic example from several years of architectural composition: the winding path through small clumps of trees that never quite congeal into a wood and never quite open up into a field, finds itself attaching (but not quite announcing) a series of buildings that it 'comes-upon'. They themselves may well turn their back upon this path, or more likely agree to offer the occasional clue of their respective purpose or physique. A game of 'did she smile at me or not and where did she go?'

I frequently read the works of CP Snow – a 40s and 50s person who succeeded in pointing out the trace of villainy and tactlessness in his heroes and the near-reasonableness of his villains as well as the tellingness of the apparently ordinary situation and the relative emptiness of the big set-piece event.

In my own architectural pieces (so far mostly 'paper architecture', but mostly buildable) I am consciously torn by the inspiration of other cultures in architecture where there is a very definite statement and a clear point of departure and the enjoyment of the English waywardness.

One resolution is to set up a clear game at the outset and then pick away at it – pick, pick, pick – until it is about to fall apart, but not quite. If you can get it right, it must be magic. All is not what it seems; there is more than meets the eye. The essential time-space characteristic of architecture makes it possible. From this viewpoint it is inevitable that I am attracted by the qualities in much Gothic architecture (forgetting for the moment the 'technic' nature of that architecture): the entry into a space in which you cannot see all, peering through the merest gap for a glimpse of a possible space beyond; turning through space which is moreover affected by changes of light and sequence.

I don't think Bruckner's symphonies are boring. True there is plenty of repetition, and you come to wait for the dropping of the third clarinet on the third near-variation. But in such music there is the hint of a hint of a hint of a possible alternative melody that might be reconstructed out of the present one, if Mr B had even more time and even more orchestral resources. Sibelius inverts the typical symphonic method by offering a series of hints and segments of the ultimate theme; he plays with these hints in a mixture of brooding melancholy and saucy dismissiveness (the Finns are, after all, great alcoholics) and then amazes you by wrapping the whole thing up at the end. Architecture has learned plenty from the flat arts – especially in the early part of this century – but it can learn plenty from music, and not only in terms of dry, methodological composition as such. More still in terms of twisting and turning, easing and intensifying, hinting and reminiscing, stating and counterpointing.

So for me, the most tedious experience is listening to folk music: the note heard raw and clear. The most tedious experience is the architect who sticks to the rules. Knowing the rules is useful – but so as to be able to tear them almost to smithereens. The most tedious reasoning for a building is that it makes all those references. The eye, ear, nose, hairs on the back of the neck – they are very reliable antennae . . . let us make them sing and twitch. Don't worry if people think that you are a bit of a sensualist and not much of a clever scholar. Old Lutyens (or was it Paganini?) just winked then, I think.

Peter Cook, August 1986

'STOREFRONT' EXHIBITION
NEW YORK 1989

Let us first examine the methodologies of architectural example and discussion, existing as they do in parallel and as counter attractions for our attention as we search for direction at this suspicion-ridden point in history. The heroic models are there for us all: as High architecture or as Obvious architecture. Cannot the Taj Mahal and a work of Louis Kahn become elevated to the same plane of recognition in time? It is perhaps our arrogance and our impatience that hustles forward the moment at which their credentials make their own contact. There surely must be a period, albeit uncomfortable, during which the coterie discussions that have drawn our attention to the Kahn item are softened into the mythology that surrounds the Taj. We are of course utterly suspicious of mere claims of beauty, and so we grow up assuming that Jefferson's Monument, the Houses of Parliament, St Basil's or Nôtre Dame are essential pillars of civilisation.

Architecture represents the unconscious acceptance of historical consequence with all its pain, greed, unfairness and chance. If however, we come to overhear a small voice making less than soothing noises about these worthies – maybe calling attention to an inconsistency or a crassness of line – we suffer a hurt not dissimilar to that of a proud and protective parent hearing ill of his child. We either shy away from such cynicism or insolence; or perhaps we are architects and join in with relish. Surely we will pick away at the bourgeois acceptance that the Great are necessarily Good.

From this point onwards it might be said that architectural criticism begins its long walk away from life – or at least from that liberal and tolerant view of life that knows (and forever after assumes) that all is not what it seems: that the same inconsistency mixed with myth mixed with hyperbole mixed with laziness informs the reliability of media News, the reputation of a restaurant or the ability of a performer. Overlaid is the dangerous geography of taboos that are particular to architecture. These ebb and flow as the result of societal change and the changing view of history – or so we would like to think – but are equally the playthings of boredom and immediacy. Taste and aesthetics are the stuff of this ebb and flow just as the catchwords and body signals of their bearers.

Architectural criticism has also to reconcile itself to the inconvenience by which it is necessarily bound to a long-winded, messy and often circumstantial operation: namely that of building. If only the cut and thrust of architectural politics and valuation could stay in the abstract, I seem to hear. If only the linguistics and the mathematics could be pure. If only the waywardness of these children who suddenly decide to drag the hand on the pencil into an unexpected – and oh so inconsistent – condition would desist.

At a certain stage, then, the critics prefer to speak only to each other and relegate that greatest part of architecture to the category of the merely operational buildings in which we often find ourselves living, working or thinking of other things. Along with all this, there are the survivors of innocence. The survivors of ignorance, indulgence – but sometimes luck – who make buildings as they feel them, caring to fly in the face of criticism or the mode of the day. Irritatingly committed as such architects often are, their works serve as a clue to the ultimately unexplainable; the whole notion that designing by drawing involves so many series' of overlaid syntheses that they could never be talked through. Nor could they ever be properly categorised.

The recent history of attraction to architectural drawings *per se* has the unhappy task of picking a path between the quicksands of invention (for on a flat drawing one can be inventive – happily, dreamily and relatively quickly) and the temptations of pattern. Many afficionados of the architecture gallery or magazine have become obsessed by technique: by the succulentness of a dramatic shadow, by the aridness of a regularly repeated line, by the titillation of the nearly illiterate (but totally controlled) piece of mechanism such as an Escher-like exercise, an axonometric viewed from beneath or a machine that might rotate if only we could identify the paths of pivotality.

Finally, we have the tragi-comedy of making architecture as a self-conscious banner or totem held up in order that the afficionados will nod and wink, the unwary will follow and the uninspired will uselessly sneer: rhetorical architecture (though it can often take on a quiet-seeming form); allegorical architecture (though it can sometimes be unwittingly imitated – and built! – perhaps by a follower) and experimental architecture (with all the potential hazards of the experiment that exploded, or failed . . . but the outside chance that the by-products of the experiment are more telling than the original intention).

Having presented these parallel conditions, I am now ready to pass out a few small clues about the work that Christine Hawley and I have been doing during the last year or thereabouts. I am, as you see, hyperconscious of the funny world in which it finds itself. I am also realistic enough to know that it is itself the curious child of several of these strands working together.

After all, we have both been working as teachers for a very long time. We have both been operating as uncle, aunt, ally, irritant, cajoler, hypnotist, foreman, diver, cat-stroker for hundreds of other architects who are in our 'care' for a short while. In doing this we begin to develop amazing antennae that detect fear, blandness, wit, caution, craft and all those ways in which we choose to expose them or wrap them up in a pastry of sophistication. People tell us that we are both very good critics. The danger of this is that you can pre-edit every move that you might make yourself in the same way that you have just post-edited those of another. I suspect that it is a certain laziness in both of us that has prevented this; the laziness mixed with the arrogance mixed with the pleasant sensation that one gets from seeing something juicy on the paper that drops all the criteria of conscience and all the chat in favour of that bit of scribbling. The same laziness (which can of course be conveniently allied to a discussion of 'English pragmatism-empiricism-literary inconsequentiality' as an excuse) applies to our delight in shifting ground on our theoretical position.

What, then, is our theoretical position? On theory itself: that it is useful if it leads – and pretty directly – to a better informed building. It is useful if it aids literacy regarding parts, or regarding the logicality of interdependent features of a design. We are both irritated by the uninformed mind and delight in lateral thought, but we also have a healthy suspicion of the overloaded mind. On architecture itself: that it is the ultimate proof. There is no substitute. Drawings, discussions, even this lovely publication are mere sidesteps around the real issue. Every drawing within is wanting to reach out and touch you, shade you, lift you, enclose you, echo back at you. Like many of our friends we want to build. On experiment: as you might have guessed, these projects are categorised as experimental architecture. They are less concerned with demonstrating the deviations or exercises built up around a serial hypothesis than in demonstrating the cumulative effect of like piled upon unlike, the cumulative effect of architectural invention that suggests alternatives even to itself. Let me demonstrate this with reference to drawing. In the Peckham scheme, Christine chooses to rework a sectional drawing in pencil, after the ink drawing at a smaller scale, has been made. The later drawing abandons certain artefacts and, as it happens, moves towards a calmer aesthetic than in the original 'scribble'. It is as if the eye and mind are arguing within themselves and willing an editorial effect upon the scheme. At this point the fact that it is a drawn exercise almost gets in the way, for the editorial effect (in this case 'calming') is both intellectually and creatively a *fluid* state. In such a way so many architects are still to be found fiddling with details while the edifice is already under construction. As a clue, Christine likes nothing better than being 'down' on the building site, persuading the craftsman and choosing the bricks.

On this same point, I can refer of course to several parts of my 'Way Out West' project which is all to do with the constant metamorphosis of substance. The drawings act as cartoons logging the occasional moment in the relentless process of transmogrification – admittedly, along a *general* direction towards the looser from the tighter – but do not be surprised if the thing were to partially tighten again. What happens to that substance itself is one thing, (to me, fascinating), but what happens regarding the whole physiognomy of skeletons and paths and veins and eruptions as time goes on is almost impossible to draw anyway.

What is our theoretical position concerning the state of architecture? Somewhere between despair and wonderment. For, just when you are so fed up with the flatness and paper-thinness of Post-Modernism, there comes a dramatic and arch-politicised shift towards the architecture of our talented friends who carve things out of space, have a natural eye and enjoy the mechanics of action. Yet as soon as they are identified, those thoughtless wandering Wallies who read the magazines start jotting down the buzz-bits (the same as buzz-words in

conversation) and graft them onto the thoughtless lumps of city block as usual. Our position as teachers is a clue, as we search for wit and initiative and an instinct for alchemy. Coming from England we are experts in the impurity and the dynamics of shuffling along. The new architecture will come from the old, that is for sure. But it will come from the essence of the old, not from its trappings. It will come from the moment that is still best captured by the cartoon image of the baboon who has just invented the wheel standing wide-eyed under a giant question-mark. A really interesting baboon will know instinctively that it goes round and round, but will already have started puzzling as to whether it can go round the other way.

To erect a point of departure and then dismantle it is an interesting enough exercise (or philosophy), but it is still, for my taste, too puritan. What if some of the effects of dismantling choose to stick and others even re-mantle themselves. The delightful irritation of living in a large and untidy city is that you never quite know whether it will work, or whether you will bump into the same people in the street as yesterday.

In her project for Peckham, Christine starts off from a healthy-unhealthy condition. She lives nearby and her own domestic enclave is a tiny piece of early-Victorian seclusion, the houses are virtually *cottages ornées*. Yet all around is the world of high-rises, muggings, racial unease and the crushed Macdonald-pack. In a corner stands a collection of rusting metal and clawed-at wood; shuffling figures and silly laughs are its animation. To be merely sympathetic to the patina of everyday decay is not enough. In a sense, there is more to be gained from the undercurrent of violence in the community of Peckham. Its conglomeration of bijou cottages surrounded by flowers, peeling terraces of low-grade shops and assorted sheds that might at once be bus garages or cinemas or depots in which those hit-and-shoot movies thrive. In her inventions, Christine quickly re-erects the apparatus of not only slithering and sliding panels, but of creaking or even screeching metal and puts up a virtual scaffolding that invites the many ladders, stairs and leaning objects from which the shifty or scampering characters upon the scene might dart away from the cops. If I have already been cynical about the walking away of architectural discussion from life and into the world of measure, diagram and neatness of thought, I might be tempted to ascribe, by contrast, to all her energy of form and the circumstantiality of a street-wise location, the status of a populist

alternative. Yet I know that this is far from being Christine's direction. More, I think, is found in the territory of stranding or stripping of the elements. Regard, if you will, such drawings she makes as collections of nerve-endings. In this way, one can trace the jumping across from photographed (and of course frequently – almost daily – observed) fragments through an imagination that starts to animate them. 'Designing', in the sense of calling up new substances and new shapes, becomes a secondary activity.

This is not so in the case of my own project for Berlin. I will readily admit to playing a more Heroic game, setting-up as I do a whole parody of a 20th-century city in order to disintegrate it. Moreover, the scenario must include a less consistently raw set of characters, both human and material. Yet I am equally uninspired by the idea of a consistent intellectual standpoint. The shiftiness of the scheme is, I hope, much greater than any formal or physical shiftiness that I can summon-up in the drawings.

To return again to my scant survey of methodologies of architectural memory, I must admit to a love-hate relationship with the acceptance of historical consequence. The politics of change could also be expressed as a paradigm of the politics of misuse, random factors and the unrecognised. For every one spectator that lines his eye in the correct spot to enjoy the axis, the entasis or the articulation of parts, there are three who shuffle past, deep in their own thoughts – though there is undoubtedly a 'feel' to certain places. To ignore this constituency of architecture is all too tempting and can be associated with the inevitable wish of a scholar or a designer to be true to a direction or a commitment. Hence the pursuit of the 'clean' drawing of absolutely equal line thickness, lest any preference sully the discussion. To read the political vehemence and purity of Hannes Meyer and then to dissect the axonometric of his League of Nations project is to enjoy his power of thought (both verbally and physically) but be irritated by statements such as:

> Building is a technical and not an aesthetic process, artistic composition does not rhyme with the function of a house matched to its purpose. Ideally and in its elementary design our house is a living machine. Retention of heat, insulation, natural and artificial lighting, hygiene, weather protection, car maintenance, cooking, radio, maximum possible relief for the housewife, sexual and family life etc are the determining lines of force . . .[1]

Without becoming enmeshed too far in an anti-functionalist reaction, we can see that there is something coldly analytical about this picture of living. Something that (whatever the aesthetic) would eliminate the twigs and tweaks of form in the Peckham scheme and would probably completely demolish any of the bulges and deformations within the Way Out West story.

Yet we ourselves chose to apply a certain consistency to the drawings, a certain style of object, a certain aesthetic preference. In a sense, the 'feel' of our buildings would be their own feel. The kind of light that is to be permitted – or encouraged – within the space of a typical room in the skyscraper for Way Out West would be the product of the ambiguous state of its 'play'. In the early stages (A to C) the room will reflect the discipline of the post-and-beam structure operating at five-metre intervals. The gradual shift of the glass in relationship to this will begin to challenge the authority of the structure and (hopefully) start to set up two conditions of light. But later still, as stages D and E emerge, the stability of reference will begin to vary, so that the occasional vertical frame or completely transparent window will serve as reminders of an age when all was what it seemed. My instinctive memory is of Gothic space and of Gothic devices.

In the best kind of Gothic cathedral, the altar area is almost hidden from the nave by a screen. If there are permitted apertures through the screen, they are concerned with the temptation of space rather than the explicit revelation of objects. Similarly, the condition of light that is transmitted via a vaulted ceiling from clerestory windows that are almost out of sight (the monastery at Jasna Gora near Cracow being my most recent reminder) is somehow more luminous and more effectively a foil to the specifics of the various objects seen below. This separation of architectural condition and architectural object is too often forgotten by the easy way in which we feel that we must make, place, delineate and specify a device and then have a clear emanation from it. Light? Use a window. Move? Use a stair. Heroicise? Use an axis. Relate? Use a horizontal line. Separate? Use a wall.

The difficulty is that our old Pillars of Civilisation (Jefferson, St Basil et al) are considered to be sufficiently circumstantial that the chatter of history is the creation of mystery enough. To approach the same issue from another direction, one only has to remember the frustrations of the 1950s and 1960s architects: having discovered the Italian hill towns and the notion that agglom-eration of time was at least analogous to the agglomeration of architectural nooks and crannies (not to speak of aesthetic looking skylines), they were desperate to reproduce these qualities in brick, concrete and heavily-shadowed drawings. The early Bofill building called Xanadu might be considered as an example of this. So too might the much more recent Yamamoto International building by Hiroshi Hara, where the play of intermittent form recalls the work of a very clever player of scrabble. The frustration remains because the time factor lends levels of inconsistency to the fabric that are inexplicable by shifts of style, changes in the size of brick, deviations in the recognition of heroic or humble space.

It may be noticed that neither the Peckham project nor Way-Out-West seem to encourage the retention of high-profile as an important ingredient of their imagery. Both schemes seem to home in on the cross-section, both schemes seem to be as interested in the occasional appearance of an element or a device that is almost inciden-tal – maybe a piece of apparatus or a piece of localised structure or a hint of a soft surface – rather than the icon. Earlier work was more iconographic. In the Porchester Baths of 1980, Christine accentuates the columns before allowing sensuous twirling drapes to carry the eye away and around them. In the Archigram period of my own work, though probably naughty and con-sciously anti-architectural, a Thing is a Thing: an anti-house is still a complete object; or, as in the case of the 'Control and Choice' project of 1968, it is made up of a series of identifiable and self-possessed items – 'The Car', 'The Robot' and so on. And for the observer, I have no doubt that the sharp-featured nature of an iconographic assem-blage is very convenient. Let us suppose that Christine was willing to state her project as 'an essay on the mobility of panels', or as 'the agglomeration of new ways with scaffolding', or that she retained a strict order of form based somehow upon the growth patterning of trees and wood – all would be plain sailing. One could concentrate upon measuring whether one liked, or found appropriate the hierarchical role of the bits and pieces within the frame of reference.

In my own work, I suspect I have less ability (or less wish) to abdicate the occa-sional usefulness of hierarchical sequences and their attendant iconographic players: the King, Queen, Castle, Knight or Pawn are an amusing cast of characters . . . particularly if you discover that the humble Pawn in stages A and B starts to exert himself and becomes a power in the land by the time of stage D; whereas the Queen is but a Queen and the troublesome old Castle sits around getting (usefully though) in everyone's hair through-out the game. Such are my regards for the roles played by Matrices, degrees of shift and paths of influence as well as the joyous and slightly frightening story of the growth of the cactus family. As far as the cactus is concerned, if I try to explain it too specifically, I wrap myself up in an unnecessarily tight corner. It carried my thoughts forward in two different ways: as (almost corny) symbol of the desert and the American West; and then as the reminder of a physical formation that has repeatable, envelopable skin character-istics, but with those intriguing and potentially technological prickles that start to talk about scale and facility and contact. It served me anyhow, although as the scheme moves forward the simple cactus form is necessarily evolving into something more reminiscent of extruded chewing-gum or the product of a powerful spray gun. Once again, the exam-ple of history is that innovation has been the servant of necessity. There is a tiresome theory that the major thrusts forward are created by extreme situations of war or flood or fire. The 1938-45 war forced the pace of glued-timber technology and the develop-ment of plastics to such an extent that the raw basis of the cactus can be found in its history. The wisdom of Warren Chalk's research for 'Archigram 6' was in ascribing to the 1940s a creative role vis-à-vis architec-ture that is fundamentally far beyond the identifiable heroics of 'l'Esprit Nouveau' or the 'Festival of Britain' which flank it.

In choosing their own ground, we must accept that our projects will be read as having a didactic purpose and we would be naive to shy away from this responsibility; we would be dishonest anyway. The avoidable danger lies, however, in allowing a looseness of explanation to reduce the number of useable messages. In other words, they are to be read as both walking away from 'acceptable' architecture in order to 'walk towards life'. The suburb of Peckham could be replaced by a new community – the troublesome inhabitants decanted and 'steadies' moved in. Alternatively, an over-view on what might 'be good for them' could be arrived at. (In fact, this is what happened in the 1950s, and the resultant architecture is, in its own right, quite elegant – though physically abused.) As a more likely alterna-tive – by default rather than anything else – the existing fabric, a laissez-faire mixture of this and that, can be variously inhabited and patched up. The old premises of Montagu Burton's clothing emporium (giants of the 30s designed in the Russian Palace style) has become Macdonalds. And who cares?

The Berlin project chooses to deal with humanity a little differently. I was inspired by the absurdity of Berlin, just as much as by the necessity for it to continue with its positive survival. That so many witty, creative and original people chose to stay there – when elsewhere, they could have better facilities and country cottages near at hand is a testimony in itself. But another Berlin resides in the pages of John le Carré as much as in those of Christopher Isherwood or the songs of the Threepenny Opera. The most difficult element to design – or even to characterise – is the 'underworld': that part of the scheme in which the outcrops that start in such an orthodox manner and end so wantonly are bedded down . . . and are never in any clear-cut relationship either to each other or to any notion of 'figure ground'. For many years I have been more than cynical about the value of 'figure ground'. The idea that a building is either there or not there is altogether more crude. But the 'deck' is equally crude. At least conceptually, an ideal state would be a combination of the idea of the intertwined roots of the lower levels and a vision of space between buildings allowing the occasional outstretched arm or frantic wave, so long as this can also have the incidental quality of the spontaneous gesture. Simple arms and legs thrust out between towers was sufficient for Sant' Elia of Archigram, but not now.

One likes to imagine that a very mixed bag of people live in the city that replaces the derelict railway yards behind the Hallensee. At the moment, the area possesses a slightly creepy air. The gentility of the Grünewald suburb is straightforward enough, as is the other patch further North where the giant Congresshalle and Tower make adequate use of blank patches of gash land – so long as one is not in any way concerned about urban grain. The mixed bag thrusts up from the Kurfürstendamm and anyone who has watched the constant parade of the ambitious, the pretentious, the colourful, the pragmatic, the waspish, the predatory and the very normal along that special street will immediately understand. The trees and cacti, the smooching, swaying skins and the commodiously organised spaces will reflect them all. I should like my buildings to be unevenly inhabited. I should like the effect of sweeping 'greenswards' – these small, contained parks, to be the preference of a certain (dare I say 'bourgeois') Berlin type. I should like the under-areas to be activated by a lifestyle just this side of legal.

I wrote near the beginning about the survival of architectural innocence. I suspect that I have exposed a parallel craving – for the eschewement of social and cultural innocence, but perhaps exposed at the same time a sympathy for the condition of architectural innocence. Up to this point, I have studiously avoided the use of the word 'Expressionism'. Partly because I feel that it has too often been used to describe a relatively narrow territory of architectural taste – and we have to be particularly careful about this within the context of Germany. But I have also been avoiding it because of its over-directness of mechanism. I am not attracted to the idea of an architecture of the jerked knee. It is the equivalent of the 'light-use a window, territory-use a door' conversation. At an earlier time I used to think that the mere invention of an additional vocabulary of form might cure many ills. If there can be a series of additional devices listed-out for the purpose of illuminating a room beyond that of the window – up to and including the use of incandescent light, lasers, mirrors, tricks of light and tricks of section – so well and good. But increasingly I find myself asking the question: so we always want light? And should it be soft light, strong light, immediate light and . . . for goodness sake . . . could it not be remembered or *imagined* light?

The most exciting discussions that Christine and I have ever had about architecture may well have occurred around the time that she was designing her 'Shadow House'. It certainly acts as a model for contemplating the relative roles of organisation, memory, object and icon. Its hypothesis was that a series of architectural parts might well have to exist, but certainly did not necessarily have to announce themselves to the spectator, or the wanderer through the building. Indeed, some of them might only be glimpsed as seductive shadows or suggestions of the presence of the object. Others might deliberately distort and (as it were) shy away from you on your approach. The whole attitude towards territory was to run parallel to this . . . so that the delineation of space would certainly not demand a wall . . . maybe only a mist, or a mesh, or a curtain, or (and this is the difficult stuff) an impingement by other surrounding devices. Of course, the essence of this exists in the classical language of architecture: how else do we accept the role of the propaeleum, the sequential game played by the Assyrian temple or the aperture in the Pantheon? As a clue, it is not without chance that the plan form of the Shadow House takes a neoclassical footprint

as its point of departure.

In my own work, the 1972 project called 'Urban Mark' sets up the scenario for redefining context and the idea of continuity into an alternative, shifting perspective. Once again, the simple, classical mark is there – this time the intersection of two lines and the deification of the point of that intersection. The traditional (one might almost say the biological) attachment and the sustenance of the supporting parts to the given armatures is direct and obvious. But what is less consequent is the series of shifts that occur once the thing has begun to deregulate and slurp around. Eventually and inevitably the organic mass abandons the cruciform frame. In parallel, the parts abandon their family roles . . . though it may or may not be significant (and the scheme was made a while ago) that in the last of the sequenced drawings there is something in common with the 'moon-like' landscape. 'Drift' seems to have emerged as a key word here. 'Tweak' might be another. 'Slope' and 'Slurp' and 'Hint' and 'Slide' can be added. They suggest and confirm our antipathy to the formal and locked architecture that we see in so much of America, England or Germany, in that they are essentially dramatic – that is, to do with the nature of the action and some scale of gentleness or brutality – and there is a richer territory that we are naturally tempted by. To describe this as having to do with theatre is considered (at least in the non-expressionist, non-Latin world) highly suspect. Woolly. Corny. Perhaps it has useful connotations though, with life itself. We both admire the ability of most citizens of Glasgow to describe the most commonplace events of the day in anecdotal language that is not only colourful and descriptive but just on the acceptable edge of imagination that touches upon fantasy. Now such a description of a circumstance is not a bad model for architecture itself, Is it not?

If our projects crave to relate to the vicissitudes of life itself, they do so in a very positive way. This edge of imagination in the Glaswegian narrative is a little heady and certainly gains momentum in the act of telling a story. Hopefully, the restrictions of our own architectural style have no more significance than the same mixture of charm and deflection that comes from the dialect of the Glaswegian voice.

Notes
1 Hannes Meyer, *Die Neue Welt*, 1926.

THE ARCHIGRAM EFFECT

What continues to amaze me is the apparent ease with which Archigram developed from a serious, but modest, basement 'tease' concocted by some rebellious young architects to deliberately irritate the 'neat' and 'boring' and 'superior' fellow-workers in a respectable series of London offices . . . and continued, despite the British system of putting down . . . namely, total lack of interest . . . to become a world-famous phenomenon.

We genuinely never felt like a phenomenon, but maybe we simply had nerve?

Nerve is what it may well be about. I write this having just, last night, heard Shin Takamatsu give his first lecture outside Japan. Now he has nerve. I'm not too sure whether I love or hate his buildings. I don't know whether to laugh or cry, but I certainly cheer and clap the loudest. Rather him a hundred times than those awful, weedy, careful, 'let's look over-our-shoulder-and-see-if we're doing the right thing' types. Anticipating the BIG SWING that they are going to have to make with Philip Johnson giving 'Deconstructivism' the OK, I am filled with anticipatory giggles. They're going to have a terrible time, for, unlike with Post-Modernism, it is difficult to do. In the early 1960s these same 'types' were the people that we deliberately taunted and ultimately hoped to threaten with our *Archigram* broadsheet.

We had each studied in different schools and really had very different tastes and, as is well documented, the ultimate Archigram Group was the combination, more or less, of two separate groups. It was perhaps its strength that Mike Webb's ability to learn to play Brahms or hum long passages of Wagner had little to do with Dennis Crompton's understanding of engines, or Warren Chalk's involvement with American painting. The overlap was an enjoyment of teasing: teasing the architectural extremity and most of all the architectural language.

Strangely, though, I still find myself fascinated by the question, 'Why is the language of architecture so limited? Why does it, historically, move forward a few centimetres in range, only then to have to retreat back a metre until, in 30 years' time, it creeps forward a bit more?' Probably the most exciting new name in the last 10 years, Santiago Calatrava, is still uncomprehensible to most (even intelligent) architects who have

to stress his significance as an engineer (therefore in a mysterious but measurable territory), rather than face up to the fact that he is extending and offering a new series of discoveries for architecture. They never understood Bruce Goff for the same reason.

The Archigram effect upon me was to superimpose an even tougher, more competitive and more psychologically challenging Academy over my present day-to-day life than even the AA school (which then as now was pretty daunting itself). Amongst fellow believers and fellow conspirators you only put out a signal if it was useful to 'the Attack'. Otherwise you stayed silent. The signal in this case had to be a drawing. The drawing had to engage with the drawings of the other members of the group. Unlike school, office or architectural competition, the drawing did not waste time in accommodating irrelevant criteria, fighting-off unwanted attacks; it could concentrate and it could comment positively upon the others' drawings.

It is therefore no accident that Warren Chalk's 'Capsule Homes', Ron Herron's 'Walking City' and my own 'Plug-in City' were absolutely simultaneous. They clearly had something to say to each other. Often it was Webb who was ahead – I still regard him as the most incredible of us all – yet we then responded to the suitcase-as-house or the warmed-up egg or the cloud-as-dreams environment each in our own way.

The drawings changed in style and here one was more directly influenced than one might have been in a formal Academy. My line got thicker because Ron, Warren and Dennis drew with thicker lines and – my God! – it worked! It looked like something in reproduction (even reduced to 4 cm on bad newsprint it looked like something). I suppose that this case reveals an arrogant desire on the part of us all to make our position felt, in magazines, in galleries and inevitably, as teachers. We were conscious of the avant-garde of Europe. We felt very much part of a continuous line from Mies, Gropius, Taut and Corb, through to the bombast of CIAM. Through CIAM to TEAM 10. That got closer: Webb had been taught by Stirling, Greene by Bucky Fuller and I by Peter Smithson. The other half of the Group had met with the Independent Group of English artists and architects. There it was.

'Let's have another look at that catalogue, Ron, . . . hey! They were dangling mobiles in Stuttgart in 193- . . . Hey, if we make it out of foam it'll do that thing Moholy-Nagy was on about . . . Or something like that.'

Occasionally, just occasionally, we felt exposed. That dreadful and particularly English diffidence – the calculated lack of interest – must have a generic relationship with the equally calculated Tradition of the English Eccentric. Why otherwise did I first observe the Smithsons? Because they wore funny clothes: silver, lemon yellow, loud check. It had to be them and their funny houses. Just occasionally, the disdain of the sub-Brutalists (the bright young men who hung around Stirling, Gowan and the Smithsons – who were already names around Town) got on our nerves. 'Come on', we thought, 'We're not the Enemy, we're just trying to chivvy things along a bit, say Hello!' They didn't, yet they were talented and interesting. But over time I have observed this phenomenon in other cities: the greatest danger to the forward movement lies not in the dozy, untalented, naturally provincial mass of architects, but amongst the informed but self-satisfied in the main cities. Unfortunately, this includes many English teachers in architecture schools: many interpreters who have little visual sense and not a few German and American professors.

The little magazine cannot be kept out of your letterbox. A school of ideas can exist outside a school of architecture. I think that is why we kept the magazine going for 10 years. At mid-point in its history, the magazine *Architectural Design*, which was edited by Monica Pidgeon with Robin Middleton as her deputy, hosted a fantastic team of encouragers and informed critics. We were noticed and supported by Reyner Banham who wittily kept us at needle point; he and Cedric Price becoming the necessary 'conscience' and 'sage' figures.

Somewhere in the process it became obvious to us that we were becoming famous – at least in Banham's characteristic phrase, 'famous to 230 people throughout the world'. Strange letters started to arrive from Prague and Florence and Oulu. Invitations to exhibit and to lecture emerged. Precisely how this affects the pitch and thrust of the work is difficult to explain but it is probably critical.

The internal exchange, as I have explained, could use visual as well as verbal hints and passwords. For outside consumption the hints and passwords had to be more explicit. Moreover there is the consciousness of a total Archigram output to be considered: the increasing public for our work (it soon reached more than 230!) seemed to expect bright colours and rounded corners and machines that could go 'bang' in the night. Self-parody is a problem with all architecture whether hot or cool.

In fact, few of the shapes and the objects themselves seem important now and I have the suspicion that I might return to using a rounded corner or two at any time – having got over the self-consciousness of so many memories associated with the form. Similarly, I might want to use a mobile element or two . . . in fact I am, in the current 'Way Out West' scheme for Berlin. It is in the range of ideas that were suggested by the Group and reinforced by project after project – almost creating a series of mega-projects that were made from the close-packing of project over project – that I now dwell upon the Effect of Archigram.

The most important effect has been to build up a motivation, or internal power to any piece of work. A feeling that it is going to be useful in its own right – however weird or unprogrammatic it might be (the very opposite of many efforts on the part of European competition-enterers who look over their shoulder so hard to see whether they are doing the right thing). Collectively we knew that we were not doing the 'right' thing at all! Perhaps though, the vegetational shift in the work did emerge at the time when ecology-talk was in the air. Perhaps the softening of forms did occur when the space race had begun to be an inescapable part of popular culture. This raises the question as to whether Archigram was essentially to do with escape – escaping forward perhaps?

There is a terrible tightness around European architecture that is the product of history, closely populated activities, an over-concern with tradition and much else. Archigram is still for me a symbol of defiance against all of that. The great collective shrug. Occasionally the great collective rude finger sign. The Archigram effect is that of dare and of watching how other architects are sometimes encouraged to find that it is possible to innovate, to turn a programme on its side, to fly in the face of local traditions or local inhibitions.

In the present context it is inevitably a piece of detective work to see which elements of a project are affected by the accumulated ideas thrown up by the Archigram Group. I cannot draw a division – Fuller and Kahn and Le Corbusier and Taut and the unknown inventors of gadgets are there as honorary Members of the Archigram Group (if you like). In other words, one carries one's own preselected reference system around. Of later projects, the Arcadia City is clearly a programmatic successor to Plug-in City, as is Skywaft City a successor to the Sponge series. The 'Way Out West' project is concerned with metamorphosis – as were the early projects 'Addhox' or instant villages and so on. The 'hulk' element of the 'Real City' is (I suppose) a megastructure – and certainly the evocativeness of the word 'City' in so many titles has its own lineage.

The Archigram effect has been to instil a mood of optimism so that, however it turns out, a piece of work will not actually worry too much about justification.

This article first appeared in 'Peter Cook 1961-89', A+U, *Extra Edition, Tokyo, 1989 and 'Cook and Hawley', special feature,* El Croquis, *July 1989*

THE LONDON EFFECT

I never forget that I am a Provincial.
I must never forget that I am a Provincial.
In so doing, there remains a chance that I
might avoid provinciality.

Of course, I am using this observation as
both a fact and a metaphor. My hatred and
fear of provinciality may be read as a hatred
and fear of the narrowing process; that same
narrowing process that the tradition of
Archigram stood out against. Allied to it is a
false sense of satisfaction with what goes on
and a feeling that there is no need to seek
any further set of references than those
agreed to by certain chosen authorities
(habits, clever persons, worthy causes and
the like). Allied to this is an unofficial ranking
in which the syndrome will appoint a 'major
local figure' (alive or dead) as the yardstick
and then surreptitiously appoint the 'best
interpreter', 'cautiously amusing critic',
'enemy figure' and 'prince-inheritor' (who may
or may not be the same as the *enfant
terrible*). It is most extant in architectural
cities of the second rank, such as Karlsruhe,
Bristol, Boston and Rotterdam, where the
thinness of layering of all enterprises – one
newspaper, one orchestra, one critic, one
story-line – is the real fault.

Historical accident meant that my nearest
centre was big enough and the precise
moment of entry (late 1950s) portentous
enough to avoid the trap. London has
retreated somewhat from its heroic position,
but it still contains sufficient layers of people
believed to exist in the city that you can never
know when one of them or several of them
might come through the door.

If Archigram people knew that the old
Independent Group members: the
Smithsons, Paolozzi, Hamilton, Stirling, might
glance from time to time at what they were
doing, so too did the embryo Cook and
Hawley Partnership carry out its first competition drawings with the Krier Brothers, Colin
Rowe and Buckminster Fuller literally looking
through the door. I believe that the young
Christine Hawley's only meeting with Marcel
Duchamp was from up a tree with Hamilton's
daughter; in the same way that Cedric Price
was employed as floor-sweeper at the 1965
'This is Tomorrow' exhibition. But these are
the best ways to get to know. Better, perhaps, than the selfconsciousness of the

'working group'.

An inspiration in itself arose from the
foreknowledge that my own teachers, Gowan
and Smithson in particular, were being talked
about and mimicked all across Europe. To be
referred to (in Philip Drew's Book) as the
Third generation seemed to be a distinct
advantage, for the ongoing tradition of
audacity had already been established.

As much as this, however, the London
Effect is to do with the tradition of calculated
indifference and assumed superiority of
culture. Despite thinking that they hide their
arrogance, the English display it every bit as
much as the French or the Swedes. The lack
of pronounced pieces of rhetoric to accom-
pany an assumption serves only to irritate
others the more. As an experience, to be
dealt with and battled through it is a very
effective method for separating the weak
from the strong. In the end, if you have
something to say you will experiment succes-
sively with a squeak, shout, bleat or whimper
until someone is listening. In the case of
Archigram, a pop-up book and a rounded
corner. In later work, the very fact of surviving
and coming up with yet another possibility –
balloon to hedge, shadow to mirage, filigree
fan to cactus – becomes in itself a credential.

The institutions themselves range from the
very old and essentially latent: the Royal
Academy, where one shows drawings as the
only point of contact with the provincial
bourgeoisie (in the hope that the one in
l0,000 eccentric provincial bourgeois might
want to build a Shadow House or Shadow
Dog Kennel); the Architectural Association
which has always known it was the best and
in so doing has become the best; invented
institutions like Art Net, where a millionaire
offered me six years – no more, no less – to
hold exhibitions, rallies, symposia, lectures
by anybody that amused me at the time.
They inevitably amused more people too, but
the institution itself was merely a piece of
drifting collage. The London effect is to take
such institutions in its stride and not feel
nearly as threatened as New York would be
by the wayward and sometimes impercepti-
ble rules by which each of them operate.

Similarly, the London effect is to offer up
young talent continuously. If interesting, this
talent will be given house-room, platform-
room, wall-room along with the rest, but

equally, it will then be imbued with frustration
and lack of financial support along with the
already famous.

The architectural ebb-and-flow that is
represented by the last two or three decades
in London is marked by the retreat from
Modernism that was already being discussed
by Nikolaus Pevsner in some lectures in the
mid-1960s and was then commentated upon
by Reyner Banham in some *Architectural
Review* articles of the same period. The
retreat has passed through more defused
layerings than it might have done in a more
vitriolic culture, South America or a more
philosophically-based culture, say France. In
England, the positions taken by people are
often implicit and declarations of position are
rare. Positions emerge: we knew of the
embryo building for engineering at Leicester
as it sat on the drawing board in Stirling and
Gowan's office on Regents Park . . . it looked
weird and the subsequent post-
rationalisations made by critics and historians
didn't really go far in explaining away its
weirdness, or rather its originality. The
formation, much later, of the Office for
Metropolitan Architecture – OMA – came
about because of the enthusiasm and natural
affinity of purpose of a teacher – Elia
Zenghelis and his best ever student – Rem
Koolhaas. Needless to say, they both taught
together at the AA during the formative years
of their office and out of that came the
extraordinary manifestation of Zaha Hadid.
Indeed, they also spawned Peter Wilson and
they are an inspiration by their very existence
in our own city. The AA years of Bernard
Tschumi are equally remembered – when he
experimented with social observation (the
Belfast project), dance, narrative and the
invention of dynamic-architectural notation,
fortunately turning it all towards the mature
architecture that he has more recently
demonstrated at La Villette and in the Tokyo
Theatre scheme.

The parallel existence of these people
'down the corridor' at the AA, along with more
Guru-like figures such as Banham, Dalibor
Vesely, Warren Chalk and the occasional
sortie from Colin Rowe can perhaps, be
paralleled in other cities. But wait, in those
other cities could they be shared?

In Paris or New York one would have to
take sides. It would be suspect to be a friend

of both Cedric Price and Dalibor Vesely. One would have to be seen to be lunching with one or the other. Polemical authenticity in Paris or Milan would demand both written and social assignation. Political groupings would exclude the untidiness of being seen with the wrong person or allowing oneself to be seen – horror of horrors – with someone unimportant! Only in Los Angeles do I find a similar kind of 'relaxedness' as in London, where the coming-together of unlikely companions at a bar or contrary protagonists sharing a joke about architecture is seen as positive and even likely to lead somewhere . . . but it doesn't matter either if it doesn't.

So the London effect is cumulative. In my case, very much to do with the AA and its assumption of superiority over the other schools and meeting places in London. This assumption infuriates outsiders. Yet I have to admit that a certain type of elitism can be useful. My definition for a positive form would be that the door should always be open for the talented and the witty and occasionally for the creatively uncomfortable (to remind us to check our facts and values). One of the best London examples lasted until the early 1970s: the 'open house' of Peter (Reyner) Banham and his wife, Mary. At a certain moment you were informed that they were at home on Fridays. We met Bucky Fuller, Richard Meier, Peter Blake and many others,

for the first time, as well as a constantly revolving (and random) set of London architect-thinkers. Apparently these evenings had existed since the 1950s and they enabled the essential gossip, without which no push-and-pull would exist anywhere, to be exchanged or created.

With Heathrow airport as busy as it is, and with the English language having realised the ambitions of Esperanto, you can sit on your backside in London and wait for everyone to come through. But you can do better. Whatever aspect of one's ambition or motivation it is I am not sure, but sooner or later you feel that you want to be one of the other reasons that they might pass through.

So far I have talked about cities. In the USA, or Germany, or Australia there is occasionally someone out there in a small place doing something intriguing, but in England no! Not often. So messages go from city to city. The last minute politics of Daniel Libeskind as possible saviour of Eisenman's Institute of Architecture and Urban Studies in New York, of Bernard Tschumi's Deanship at Columbia, the ironies of Zaha Hadid's meetings with developers in Tokyo, the irritations of Leon Krier in Chicago – they are all being chewed over whilst the protagonists are still fighting at the other place. The architectural world 'up-country' is, however, too depressing and too reactionary to bear

thinking about.

On the drawing-board one has a handful of people in mind: a twist of the grid and an atmospheric nuance; would Dalibor enjoy that one? A strategy for dropping plastic envelopes from the sky; what will Cedric say? A fruity profile that Ron will enjoy. Most of all a squiggle that Christine might love or hate. Apart from the last-named, it may be weeks or months before the conversation is held, and a look in the eye will indicate that the point has been made, the gesture noticed.

The existence of Alvin Boyarsky – at times persuasive, coercive, irritating – has kept London an interesting place in which to be; the audacity and sophistication of his lecture, exhibition and catalogue programme remains a reminder that some very strange bedfellows are worthy of loving, hating or competing with. His 1970s and 1980s AA operation looks forward to the 1990s when, once again, London will have a new breed of creative eccentrics who, having deliberately chosen to misunderstand the philosophies of Europe and the procedures of America (or simply having too little stamina for them), do a few daft things and ignite the London Effect.

First appeared in 'Peter Cook 1961-89', A +U, Extra Edition, Tokyo, 1989, and 'Cook and Hawley', special feature, El Croquis, July 1989

THE HAWLEY EFFECT

I could never imagine myself sitting up on some mountain (or even in an urban retreat) simply with the drawing-board and a radio play for company, producing whatever one does. The advantage of the Archigram Group was in having a constant reference and, quite simply, company. In a sense, too, my consistent parallel activity – teaching – is a highly public activity.

My daydreaming and my moments of 'coming up with an idea' occur when walking along the street (often bumping into parking meters, old ladies, children, wooden posts and the like), or waiting in an airport lounge or sitting on the toilet (once I have exhausted the Evening Standard advertisement pages). Books – of which I have plenty – are varied: I re-read the ones that have a special atmosphere for me, such as Pehnt's Expressionist Architecture, Banham's Theory and Design in the First Machine Age or Geretsegger and Peintner's Otto Wagner. Not much Vitruvius, I am afraid. I enjoy lectures by favourites – Wolf Prix, or Zaha Hadid, or Cedric Price are never boring on platform – or lectures by complete unknowns who later nearly always become significant: I trust my 'sniff' on this one, which is why I enjoy entrepreneurial lectures as well. The reasons are totally selfish. Not so much to do with the forwarding of 'local culture': I want to be chivvied into better and more exotic operation myself as a result of this exposure.

As the Archigram Group was slowly fizzling down towards total lack of work and I was starting 'Art Net' (a meeting place in central London), Ron Herron and I followed up on a suggestion from Peter Eisenman that we enter the 'Roosevelt Island' competition. We concocted a curious idea which was to have a team of three teachers (ourselves and Ingrid Morris) and six students working together. The students – John Robins, Keith Priest, Jerry Whale, Tom Heneghan, Penny Richards and Christine Hawley – were suddenly pitched into a curious wing of academe, not the traditional role of 'drawing up' for the professors but actually being part of a nine-person group. The progress of the scheme was very jolly, but the really original part seemed to be the strange, undulating moon-landscape, designed by a quiet, concentrated young lady who was known to me only as 'Ron Herron's best-ever student'.

The announcement of a another foreign competition – that year's 'Shinkenchiku' House Design which was to be judged by Richard Meier – suggested a collaboration in which vegetation and metamorphosis, landscape and constructed armatures might coalesce. The collaboration worked fast and the very different tastes – for shapes and quirks and hard profiles in my case and for gentle undulations and sudden turns of direction in Christine's case – somehow combined into an architecture that was unpredictable but homogeneous.

As with the Archigram Group, the real value of the continued co-operation, which has now lasted nearly 12 years and past two dozen schemes, is because we are different. We draw perceptibly differently, but have a similar disregard for precedent. We have different tastes, but shared enemies. We have different public personae, but have often out-dared each other.

During the 11 years we have both been teaching – much of it together – and have therefore exercised a great deal of the rhetoric or criticism or paranoia that might have been directed at each other towards the strangeness of student work.

The real Hawley effect has been architectural, bringing into focus a latent theatricality in my work; not just the noisy, colourful theatricality but more the gothic trickery and atmospherics of theatre. The real Hawley effect has also been the basic intelligence of her approach and her use of time and idea. It is very exciting to work with someone who is alternately daring – even deliberately naughty – and then calm and methodical. In joint projects we have often reversed roles somewhere in the middle of the process.

Certainly the most important projects of the post-Archigram period have been designed together: the Trondheim Library, the Berlin Housing and the Langen Glass Museum. These have all been 'laundered' in a particular way with each of us working over the other person's drawing, then discussing and modifying the laundering again. The Trondheim Library threw up the idea of 'Mesh' which we developed over time into an attitude as well as a series of devices. Meshes themselves are a special alternative to 'walls' or 'hard' territoriality. They can play games with space, measure and definition.

We have so far built only one 'mesh' building, a pavilion at the Forum Design show in Linz, but the spatial notion remains with us and leads to the idea of 'Layering'.

Christine Hawley's 'Shadow House' is a seminal project in that it poses a determined-looking organisation (with its introductory fulcrum being a conscious quotation of the Tempietto in Rome) and then folds the artefacts around it in greater or lesser conditions of definiteness. The shadows are created by objects believed to be present, but not always seen. Coming in as modelmaker-interpreter, I was conscious of the architectural argument having moved significantly forward from the obviousness and frontality of Archigram into a new, dreamier territory but one in which the same instincts of audacity were significant.

My own extension of the programme was then inevitably to see what kind of 'city' could emerge from a 'layered' approach. The Layer City used overlays of system, one upon the other and led back (via a new route) to an old preoccupation with the idea of the Three-Dimensional City.

There is a linkage between the aesthetic of the 'Green' house (one of the Landstuhl Solar Houses) and Christine's own 'Porchester Baths'. A mood of almost Edwardian or early Californian hedonism, hiding behind screens and gentle coloration, suggested an alternative to hard, harsh, cut-out elements. In parallel ran my own use of hedges and screens. The 'Arcadia' projects had been started concurrently with the beginning of the Cook-Hawley work and in a series of sorties played this newly-discussed sensibility against my glorified (half-remembered) 'Arcadian' memories of certain English provincial towns and suburbs – Letchworth, Felixstowe, Bournemouth in particular.

Memories of places in the English sensibility must include the dreary, faded, silly and untypical. Indeed, if you talk to David Greene, Mike Webb or Christine Hawley you will get old armchairs, favourite dogs, unworkable lamps, uneaten sandwiches and things-you-can-do-with-pins as the reference material – not necessarily Corbusier and the computer. We are sometimes in danger of wallowing in this, but Christine the least of all. Suddenly she will stop the conversation short with an absolutely practical, pragmatic and unarguable reason for stopping and doing, there and then.

It is one of the dangers of fame with early projects and the brouhaha surrounding events, that one might slow down and constantly reminisce. No danger with a younger, tougher architect who can nonetheless act the joker at the least expected moment. We have behaved as serious editors of each others' ideas in the Langen Museum. It strikes us as being highly architectonic; most of the conversations that it makes are a direct playing forward of its initial decisions: the light-tight box, the cut-that-becomes-armature, the calm side of the building versus the gregarious side of the building and so-on. It is so far our most 'complete' architectural statement.

It will be interesting to see whether such consensus buildings can add up to a series in their own right and to see whether this series comments in parallel to either the Christine Hawley series (Mesh, Shadow House, Baths, Peckham Housing etc) or the Peter Cook series (Arcadia, Lantern Blue, Real City, Way Out West etc). Or each to the other. Or what. In a way (as with the Archigram Group system of referring back) it forms its own Academy.

As a formidable critic and academic herself, Christine never fails to remind me that it is the building as such that is the real objective. Obviously, Archigram, in its most rhetorical moments, never forgot that either.

First appeared in 'Peter Cook 1961-89' A +U, Extra Edition, Tokyo, 1989 and 'Cook and Hawley', special feature, El Croquis, *July 1989*

COOK AND HAWLEY DESIGNING HOUSES

Christine spent her childhood and youth as a hotelier's daughter and was therefore more familiar with the joys and fantasies of long, cream corridors and the exciting underworld of a commercial kitchen than a box in which the family was an island. By contrast, I spent my childhood and youth as an army officer's son, moved to 20 'homes' in as many years and so became adaptable to whatever corner of a house, flat, mansion, holiday shack, outbuilding or hotel was assigned to me at that moment. For both of us the 'house' was, and has remained, a liberal definition to be attended quite unselfconsciously.

In England, it seems that so much house design involves the playing out of secret social symbols. The real significance of 'front room' to 'parlour' relationships has rarely been admitted on architects' drawings. The retention of facilities for non-existent servants, the multiplication of access-ways, the hierarchy of chimney opening sizes and many other quirks are clues of a silly and elitist tradition. Unfortunately, the mid-20th century has been equally guilty of narrow-mindedness. I remember reading and learning the Parker Morris Report, the recommendations of the National Building Agency, the Housing Manuals for both England and Scotland, and realising that they thinly concealed moral strictures that served as design criteria.

So the male member of the family is shaving at 7.43 am, Granny is turned at an 80 degree angle towards the TV at 7.15 pm and little Susan is up there in her bedroom (a single box-like space, probably underheated) ostensibly doing her home-work. Too bad if the bloke has a beard or prefers the macho experience of shaving (electric) whilst driving in to work. Too bad if Gran is running a profitable machine knitting business and little Sue is a chamber music freak.

Christine spent a while studying the 1920s and 1930s housing estates of Dagenham. By the 1970s these had been flexed and perverted to include back-kitchen fish 'n' chip shops, car dealing, light industry, tombs and temples; quite simply the flotsam and jetsam of human eccentricity and the tradition of freedom.

In setting the Shinkenchiku housing competition four years ago, I asked competitors to react to the issue of 'comfort' in the metropolis. For I suspect that we both enjoyed a 'comfortable' childhood. We were both, in our eccentric environments, surrounded by coming-and-going, an open-endedness of environment and the constant possibility of something different happening tomorrow.

So we have designed houses that absorb, as much as possible, the unknown factor. On the one hand, the five solar houses have to respect the physical laws of heat, light and compartmentalisation of air. In the event, Conrad Brunner (our solar consultant and mentor) was able to lead us gently into a state of respect for these principles and we began to recognise the common sense qualities of farmhouses and cottages, banks of trees, conservatories and porches, inglenooks and courtyards. On the other hand we were determined to offer more than a tricksy box for four standard West German persons.

So each of the houses has a potential for the deliberate misuse of the parts. The roofs can be gardens, the living spaces can be workshops, the bedrooms can be combined, although perhaps the north faces (solid) and the staircases (knotty) have to stay. The Beach house is for the 'double family': the noisy, younger family and the grander, quieter, older family. The Green house implies a cultured lifestyle, perhaps that of the collector of *objets d'art*, as befits the enjoyer of quaint conditions of light and the progression of pavilions.

To us, the mere notion of 'the house' is sufficiently arch or rhetorical. So there is no attempt to incorporate any analogous definitions. To us the bungalow, the cottage, the villa, the pavilion are all interchangeable.

The Shadow House is therefore a natural progression. Not only does it represent a necessary reaction to the restrictions of the competition brief of the German houses, but it is a useful step in the redefinition of a territory that is somewhere between the domestic and the corporate. At the back of my mind, I have often thought of a way of life that is neither domestic nor just public, and I do not mean a commune. Perhaps the lifestyles of the hotel, the service flat, the ocean liner, all of them having pre-1940s overtones of course, hint at a very liberal state indeed and are directly analogous to the attitudes towards space, territory and physicality that concern the design.

If we are unashamedly making architecture as an art form, and unashamedly designing buildable art-architecture, we are drawn back to our own experience of people, and the reflection that much still remains to be investigated in this business of designing houses: the man who spends the whole weekend cooking – sometimes gourmet, sometimes experimental – with military attack and the need for an industrial dimension of equipment, the girl who entertains and really enjoys the water, would she trade it all in for one, luxuriant bathroom-as-pool? And the house-as-a-tree? A childhood ideal (not just of mine, but of thousands of kids), it isn't impossible. And the glorious, encompassing, engrossing rat-hole? Isn't that what the Yellow house is all about? and the hut for he/she who doesn't want to keep chattering away to everybody all the time, a hut, sufficiently far away from the 'house' but in sight of it. Clues exist: the den, the box room, the sewing room, the nursery, the garage, the conservatory, the cupboard under the stairs; these nostalgic crannies are hints of the possible magic of the house.

I have forgotten all my Parker Morris anyway, and Chris has promised not to remind me.

THEMES

Mystery

We are faced with a paradox: architecture must survive as a communicable public art. It must be able to provide function without undue inhibition, yet it is a mythological language of memories and deliberate diversions.

So it is that the history of architectural expressionism can be seen to ebb and flow alongside the cyclical tendencies of our culture as it becomes more or less populist, or as it becomes more or less elitist. It calls forth amazing resources as it takes on the expression of an Empire, or of a retreat.

Is my predilection for an architecture of mystery to do with a natural arrogance, is it the product of a fading and decadent culture, or is it part of one's desire to justify one's effort as intensively as possible? In 1935, Frank Lloyd Wright was, 'weary of reiterated bald commonplaces wherein light is rejected from blank surfaces or fallen dismally into holes cut into them. Organic architecture brings the man once more face to face with nature's play of shade and depth of shadow; he sees fresh vistas of native creative human thought and native feeling, presented to his imagination for his consideration.'[1]

The idea of presenting architecture to the observer's imagination for consideration pays the non-architect the ultimate compliment and I believe that we should all indulge in it. However, mystery is to do with layering, with the gradual unveiling and gradual accrual of circumstances. This attitude comes close to theatricality. The Trondheim Library, for example, not only presents its constituent internal buildings for your consideration, but suggests that they are all there, lurking around the corner. It invites you to enter the building and through close involvement and exploration, to discover the precise topographical details. The Victorians understood this business of mystery very well. Perhaps they brought to the business of commercial architecture the combination of pomposity, opportunism, invention and heroism that makes the rooflight over a department store, or gateway into a railway station, an audacious reference to a heroic novel, or a wave in the direction of a prince's palace. Mysterious architecture combines some of these characteristics but presents them more

surreptitiously (and, I suspect, with the arrogance of the oblique).

There is a characteristic of English conversation that is almost impossible to explain to the non-English (and in particular to Americans). It is to do with politeness and hidden meaning. Best practised by the aristocracy, it can be detected in the presentation of apt and commonplace phrases such as, 'How nice to see you'. If you are listening hard you will know precisely how nice it was for that person to see you. If we extrapolate into architecture we are talking about subtlety, but not necessarily about the juxtaposition of parts. We are talking about nuance, about using our sensitivity and our understanding of the traditional bedding-in of a situation.

In the Arcadian City all is not what it seems. Arcady is gentle and reminiscent and tolerant, but there are mysterious things happening towards the tops of the walls and just out of sight of the end of the line of trees. There is the disappearance and the reappearance of a line of walls. There are the near-quotations. This kind of mystery reminds me of the English suburbs – the typical suburb where the houses look much the same, objecting to the man who has a blue roof or a large Alsatian dog, where all the hedges are neat, the washing out on a Monday, and so on. But look very hard and you will find the man with an Indian temple bedroom, the man with a collection of a hundred stuffed rats or the man with his wife lying dead in a cardboard box. But it is important that he appears leaving his gate at the usual time in the morning! The extraction of this latent mystery, ambiguity and layering of life is a fascinating, if difficult ingredient for making architecture.

There is also the mystery of the inconsequential, or the search for consequence amongst the apparently inconsequential. It makes one (dangerously?) more fascinated by third rate buildings than those frequently photographed, and by backwater towns and brooding atmospheres. I don't think that it becomes too dangerous because it is always challenged by one's instinct for abrasion.

Megastructures

In his book on megastructures Reyner Banham tends to emphasise their largeness as the determining factor. But to me the really

interesting thing about them lies at a more conceptual level. It is to do with the organisation of objects and with the facility for free play of objects both with a system and against a system.

The Plug-in City is a famous megastructure, but it was the possibility of 'play' that was its essence rather than the size of the whole toy. Over a period of years one looked more and more closely at the idea of the autonomous object homing in towards an ordered structure and then travelling out again. Certain analogies could thus be drawn from the projects around the late 1960s and the patterns of congealing and fragmentation that can be observed in biological or crystalline specimens.

The megastructure as a model was rendered redundant but it remained to be rediscovered with perhaps a different function. In the Urban Mark and in the Monte Carlo project, the evolving or the itinerant parts needed a megastructure to respond to – without it the process could not even begin.

So much later, a megastructure can be proposed for the 'lofts' area of the Arcadia City which contains a very attenuated hierarchy even within the supportive geometry alone (to say nothing of the variety of the fed-in parts).

I began to realise that even something as small as an orchard could be regarded as a kind of megastructure, since to a chicken wandering around the orchard the trees contain that same coalescence of energy, support, shade and food.

In a sense the Arcadia City provides a series of almost rival megastructures – some of them very complex. However, just across the street, the Sleek area provides a ruthless, stylistic carcass, with almost endless ribbons of window totally dominating the internal architecture. On the hill across the valley, the megastructure is that of the stone wall, through which the narrow fins – a kind of megastructure themselves – can protrude. In the revised version of the Arcadia riverside, the Trickling Towers are part of a system of meshes that reach, in Banham's sense, megastructural proportions. More important is the fact that the towers themselves are the rock-like force that permits all those crazy things to happen over the passage of years.

Already we can see the complementary

role being played out by the megastructure and the effects of metamorphosis. We can see the supportive role of the megastructure if we wish to incorporate physically the potential of layering, and we can observe that perhaps the most sophisticated of mega-structures can create situations of mystery.

Casual Monumentalism

One is beginning now to explain one's architectural approach as a series of con-flicts, paradoxes, or interdependencies. It has, until very lately, been unfashionable to consider monumentalism as an aspiration, yet surely this too is an instinct to which I have to admit. But in suggesting a casual monumentalism I am probably returning once again to the predilections of the English bourgeois romantic.

In his book *Architecture and Utopia* Manfredo Tafuri discusses Piranesi in relation to the English makers of landscape grottos:

Piranesi's fragmentation is the conse-quence of that new bourgeois science historical criticism, but is also, para-doxically, criticism of criticism. The whole fashion of the evocation of Gothic, Chinese and Hindu architecture and the romantic naturalism of the garden landscape, in which were immersed the jests of exotic pavilions and false ruins, related to the atmos-phere of Montesquieu's *Lettres Persanes* and Leibniz's caustic anti-occidentalism. In order to integrate rationalism and criticism, Europeans confronted their myths with all that could confirm their validity. The romantic English garden asked for an authentication from outside architecture.

In a sense, most thinking architecture is a criticism of a criticism, but it is also character-istic of metropolitan Europeans to miss the deliberate waywardness of English design-ing. The kind of casual monumentalism is less a question of confronted iconography than an attitude about formation. Sometimes, I deliberately avoid recognisable icons since I feel that we occasionally allow literacy to take over from spirit and allow quotational cleverness to replace invention. There are joys and traps on this other side, to quote Van Doesburg:

The new architecture is formless and yet it is aptly defined. It is not subject to any fixed aesthetic form or type. It has no mould, such as confectioners use, in which it produces a functional service arising out of practicable demand. In contradistinction from all earlier types of architecture, the new

methods know no basic type, nothing is closed.[2]

In the Via Appia there is always a nagging awareness of the monumentalism of Rome and the degree to which an apparently degagé object can nonetheless present itself as a monument when facing the heroic street, and to what extent the monumentalism can be melted, and how quickly. And so again, one is using the notion of a hierarchi-cal dynamic with the climatic state of the monumental facade – somewhat in the role of the basic megastructure in one's previous argument. There is no doubt that the Arcadia City is more overtly creating its own set of monuments and, of course, these can be seen in even the most gentle and low-key English suburbs, not least when they are pretending to be villages.

The Arcadia City's peninsula contains a series of apartment blocks each one assert-ing (in the revised version) its own architec-tural style and each one contributing to a caterpillar-like total monument. But the caterpillar hugs the ground in a very furry way, the determinism of the blocks becomes less and less as they merge into the park-land. Not only is this to do with one's liking for softened edges, but it is also concerned with an instinctive notion of attack of the object upon itself. This aspect of disintegration I will discuss later.

Perhaps the peninsula, as much as the earlier Montreal Tower, and the Roosevelt Island project are all wishing to make a shrill architectural presence felt, which for me, was most effectively led in the 1960s by Hans Hollein and his landed aircraft carrier and Ron Herron and his Walking City. The earlier model is, of course, Le Corbusier's Unité d'habitation at Marseilles. Gentle monumentalism sometimes involves less perceptible tricks: the coy object, the quaint corner, the softened silhouette; these are decoys, misleading you into supposing that there may not be a grand plan, a matrix, a hierarchy, a gradual, but insistent building up of events, until you realise that you are involved in a giant vortex of organisation. This was certainly at the back of my mind in scribbling parts of the Arcadia City plan, as it has often been in the sophisticated contriv-ances of our favourite English parks.

Stourhead in Wiltshire is immensely theatrical, it evokes mystery and uses immaculate layering – even the lake might be regarded as its megastructure. Within its grottoes one finds a certain self-conscious quaintness. As a monument of operatic dimensions it has to be my favourite English place.

One must never underestimate the tendency of the English to have some devious grand plan at the back of their minds, although unlike the metropolitan Europeans they will probably forget it, or become bored by it in the more endearing process of preserving its discretion – its casualness.

Hard and Soft

A ricochet effect between elements and between stages in the playing out of a design has already been alluded to. In the 1960s there was a very dramatic confrontation between 'hardware' – the design of buildings and places, and 'software' – the effect of information and programme upon the environment. It is now so closely associated with the then current notions of urban dispersal, populism and the avoidance of finiteness of every kind that we have come to distrust its conceptual magic.

Perhaps I fall into the English tradition of the 'hugger' – the person who needs an array of props such as terrain, wall, or a certain stance towards history in order then to have an excuse to do certain daft things.

A specific physical interpretation can be the tactile quality of parts of a building. Or it can be the absorbability of its elements. Again and again I notice a tendency to coerce a 'hard' and a 'soft' condition, with the flesh of the building creating the tension between the two. Of course this flesh also contains the veins of energy emanating from both.

The street that runs between the Lofts and the Sleek area in the Arcadia City is the defining, hard line. The wall of the Loft is total, but from then on the building softens. Roosevelt Island is more obvious, and even the 'sponge' vocabulary took as its support the basic proposition that an old, hard building could be wrapped up in soft, spongy bits and pieces. There is an obvious role in all of this for preferred aesthetic elements: the creepers and layers and soft edges can make themselves symbolise the programme of the building. More interesting though is the way in which we can juxtapose 'hard' and 'soft' designing. This might mean that one chooses certain elements as needing a very determinate and consistent programme, and against this one might categorise another set as needing the greatest range of free-play. The difficulty here would be in the middle territory, but the game could be regarded as liquid megastructuring.

An alternative is to categorise the elements of a design as part of a general progression from hard through to soft, each having its own value in the scale. The danger here lies with the evaluation, but more importantly, life is never quite like that. So it could be that the worst of the old unresponsive architecture does at least have the virtue of being an established and consistent 'hard' against which the waywardness of man and his habits create a constant on-going 'soft'.

This last observation can only attract one intellectually. For the hardware inventor it avoids the issue. I suppose that I enjoy the placing of values as much as the positioning of walls. Can there be a one-to-one relationship between responsiveness and placement, or between specifics and programme? Once more it is a cultural problem . . .

Disintegration

It was inevitable that one would turn towards disintegration as a formal state if one had started out on the road past metamorphosis. I have sometimes described my recent work as 'melting architecture'. It is related to the search for or definition of a perpetual state of transition. It relates to the idea of disintegration and dissolution. It has to do with an objective notion of disintegrity – the merging of elements – and the softness of atmosphere. It implies mystery and the unexpected, but with gentleness rather than surprise.

In Arcadia 'A' there is the disintegration of the built forms as soon as you pass through the entrance. Bedford Park, an Arts and Crafts garden suburb of London and a part inspiration for that project, disintegrates in the same way. If we remember the easily recognisable state of the English street – where the facade merely hides an assortment of bits and pieces that hang out towards the backyard – Bedford Park can be considered an extreme case. The backyard has become more genteel but more crazy, and here is a clue to the relationship between disintegration and quaintness and casualness. The English like disintegration because they are short on stamina and long on individualism.

Most of the recent projects in this collection use disintegration in a straightforward way. The Arcadia Town Hall (a term which seems more evocative than 'City Hall') establishes itself at one end in the most pompous way. Its tower proclaims it to be the most important building in the city. Its consistent and gridded walls proclaim it to be the repository of an established secretariat. However, as the programme changes, the building changes – it twists and its surface fragments. The organisations within change from the monolithic to an assortment of various small and independent set-ups. The building trickles under the road and continues to disintegrate, or to formally metamorphose into a very strange kind of animal; a frag-

menting series of animal-like sheds. Other games of disintegration abound throughout the city – the aforementioned Lofts area, and the eventual state of the Trickling Towers. The placement of trees is concerned with a double formal disintegration; of building-through-to-tree, and of clumps of trees that progressively spread themselves thinner and thinner throughout the landscape. Then there is the disintegration of the Sleek area as it climbs up the hill and engages with the gentler landscape (although here we are reminded of architecture by the monumental role of the front part of the Academy). Nonetheless, the Academy itself is involved in an internal tussle between types of architecture and comes close to disintegration at its edges – columns disintegrate into sculptures and sculptures disintegrate into rocks.

My favourite food is ice-cream, and there is that fantastic moment when it has just started to melt in your mouth before the icy gulp. How does one draw that?

Notes
1 Frank Lloyd Wright, *The Future of Architecture*, Horizon Press, New York, 1953.
2 Theo van Doesberg, 'Towards a plastic architecture', *De Stijl*, no XII, Rotterdam, 1924.

ARCHITECTURE WITH A HIDDEN SMILE

Like all politics, architecture needs its shrieks and cries, its heroes and villains, its slogans and banners. The instinct of monumentality is not hidden far away, just as the wish to be liked is very near to the surface of most of us. A building seems to need to be if not liked, then admired, if not admired then understood, if not understood then heard. Cities too, seem to subscribe to the same wishes, even though cities are really more like conversational groups or crowds, with certain individuals given status or a louder voice. A parade, or a charade is played out whereby the voices are expected to be heard at a certain moment and then to stay silent: the palace at the end of the avenue is given the right to declaim loudly and majestically, often with a series of architectural platitudes, whereas, in a back street somewhere, a raunchy little building – perhaps the ill-considered extension to the washhouse – sniggers away and cares little who listens.

A few years ago, James Stirling and James Gowan (when they worked together) made observations about the nonchalance of the 'backs' of most traditional Georgian buildings in London, and the Victorian inheritors of the same set of niceties by which the street contained the well-mannered architecture, and those ragged peninsulas that form the backs contained the life-blood of the buildings (and the real dynamic of Mrs Maggs and Mrs Jones chatting to each other over the fence, hanging up the washing, keeping the odd pig, printing a Marxist newspaper or running an illicit fish and chip shop).

The cities that have received little formal planning – Cambridge, Frankfurt, Boston, Antwerp – are precisely those in which a certain ribald chatter of architecture is to be heard and where the most unlikely, but savoured memories of buildings-as-atmosphere can be found without the protocol of expectancy that is part of Paris, Washington, Berlin or Vienna.

Yet we remain a full-frontal society. In a way, buildings are rarely more subtle than the offerings of the news-stand – and in a parallel way have many similarities to each other despite their efforts to seduce our attention. The building and its neighbour indulge in a tête-à-tête with the nod of a porch and the bow of a pediment and the smile of neatly aligned windows.

When we escape to the countryside, what are we really up to? Are we purely indulging in that memory of a memory of an idea of being a simple peasant, with the freedom to chew on a piece of grass? Are we merely seeking a pictorial bliss – so long as the point of escape can still get four channels of TV? The paradox is that in Northern Europe at least, we are leaving one language of observation for another. In countryside that has experienced two thousand (who knows, three?) years of exploitation, politics, greed, invention, survival, romanticism, reasonableness, overbreeding, there is another kind of urbanism. The objects that we gaze down upon from our eyrie are natural enough in themselves: the trees, grass, wheat and water are unadulterated, as yet unprocessed – but then – are they? That hedge over there is the result of a diplomatic apportionment between the two sons of a farmer in the 19th century. That bank of poplar trees breaks the wind coming in off the North Sea and it seemed a good idea at the time. And that pond? Surely the wish of some enterprising individual to be able to water his horse without being continually polite to the Squire so that he could use his pond. And in the distance, that barren hilltop, does it not have the tradition of a jinx upon it, perhaps thought up by some avaricious monks in the 15th century so they could keep it for themselves and now transmitted by the weirdness of circumstance into a real piece of environmental eccentricity?

If we compare the number of variants upon a simple, logical analysis of the topography and its potential – as we do when we size up a piece of the city that we are putting houses upon; or if we add up the number of variants upon the placement of a tree, a hedge, a ditch, a field; as we make when we locate a window, staircase, pinnacle or gable – we might recoil in our humility. As architects, we will claim that it is our right to clarify and assert our language of objects. 'What is wrong with a door as a door as a door?' I hear the rational cry. The intervention of the two-window-one-roof building into this bucolic orchestration can blend in more easily with its sweetness and simplicity than a piece of high architecture. However, it is the sheer multi-dimensionality of the developed countryside that is the essence of its mes-

sage, for so far we seem to be using the flattest language of relationship of objects and systems when we make collections of buildings. The visual charm of this country-side should offer us a clue, because it suggests that the variety of its conditions and its charm is much to do with the scrambling of hierarchies and the suddenness of heroic situations and the unannounced incidence of the alternative device as a symphonic level of composition.

Then there is the random glance: surely the landscape designers of the 17th and 18th centuries understood well the theatrical set piece. My hunch is that in all those sketch-books of Schinkel's travels in Scotland and elsewhere, it was the casual rather than the contrived that offered him fodder for his romantic compositions. Surely it is not unreasonable to strive, at least, for an architecture that can be as responsive and as delightful? Into this we can insert deliberate decoys; the set piece of the grand house, or again, more interestingly, its formal gardens which can play a certain contrapuntal game with the nearly random part of the countryside, which can in its turn play an occasionally noted game with the really random part of the countryside. Into this we can usefully insert further set pieces: a sudden hard toy perhaps. A fixed, square, measured, paved, walled, cold, hard, rationed thing. A little building of such incisiveness that any bird that strays onto its surfaces will immediately modify its voice. In such a place all is as it seems.

After working in the Rhineland area, we have been taken to see the Maginot Line on the French side of the border several times. 'It is just like your architecture', our hosts say (referring, I think to the Via Appia/Arcadia period). And there it is indeed: the juxtaposition of high-reference objects into discrete folds of the earth. Despite the necessary observation of the horrors of war, despite the necessary irony of an extremely large and energetic system of defences that could simply be circumnavigated by any general of even middle intelligence, there is but the merest reference to what lies inside those hills. Moreover, the architecture is of a very special kind; contrived in the extreme, around certain vicious – but nonetheless – functionalist elements. They poke, probe, wink and snigger out of the undergrowth. They lurk. They masquerade as bushes. After a while, one doesn't quite know what to believe and one begins to look suspiciously at every minor reminder of formality. Two trees standing suspiciously close together: are they conspiring? That knoll in the ground: what does it conceal?

In an old project called 'Prepared Landscape' I was suggesting that a building of some sophistication could be tucked into a cleft of the rolling countryside, and could draw analogies of a formal as well as a conceptual nature between earth banks and walls, streams and slivers of metallic conditioning. It came before seeing Maginot. Now it would be even less consistent with itself.

Yet the instinct for composition remains strong and without much trouble we can invoke the eminently reasonable argument that an act of design is necessarily made at a moment and of a series of desires and that ambiguity or total scramble is impossible to sustain.

When setting up the lines of control for our Shadow House project, Christine Hawley was consciously reiterating the formality of a classical composition, with the event of the Tempietto quotation at the centre of the radial system as the point of contact with the city. The first shift of the composition, with a rival axis to the central one, was the start of a successive series of shifts and layerings of the *apparently* similar to the apparently similar. The intention of the Shadow House was related to the perceptual act of glimpsing: of seeing a shadowy form that reminds one of something known, or half-remembered; of presenting a series of leads to hidden delights, perhaps, but deliberately only disclosing some of the game to the full-frontal observer. Nonetheless, the project uses lines, paths, points of structure, geometries and containers. It attempts to scramble some of these, or to lure you away from their too obvious presentation. In doing so, the hope is to orchestrate a series of differing layers of reference – almost, to present a series of architectures together in one place, to be read or enjoyed differently and by different spectators. Inevitably, our own essentially mannered experience of being architects stands in the way of real casualness and, in the end, would we really bring ourselves to tolerate such a thing? At a certain point we will ourselves argue that there must be references.

In certain Gothic buildings, rather more than those of classical instinct, there come several coincidental moments when the reading of space and the reading of systems of objects is blurred and scrambled. Rationally, we know that regulation exists; the edifice has been here for 600 years. But what is happening to our notion of depth, what is the effect of the diffusion of the light? That statue – is it a real person, a trick of the stone, or a trick of the light? In a project for the Karmeliterkloster, Frankfurt, we attempted to design around the idea of 'glimpsing' – which at the time we thought was especially apt for a museum building, where the tradition of having hallowed objects of the past thrust at you – in full frontality – seemed unsubtle.

A predilection for meshes can be seen as a typical architects' attachment to a device that has served well through thick and thin – the architecture of the trusted friend psychology: 'I always use that stair tower, it saves a lot of bother'. Yet as we think about it, more and more it becomes a lucky introduction into the territory of the layerable reference, whereby a series of objects can be seen to have a deliberate scale and orthodoxy to themselves, most likely a grid by which they are controlled. But on a successive level there is another quite different layer. The simple superimposition of meshes that are of varying sizes and directions is the first step. In a part of the 'Arcadia City' called 'Meshed Ground', I took a riverside situation in order to make the point that the natural riverside is an ambiguous territory, not necessarily either solid ground or actual sheer water but, perhaps some soggy amalgamation of both conditions whereby the characteristics of a marsh or of a solid substance riddled by the hint of another more fluid substance can be seen as an 'establishmentally' (as well as functionally) useful device. In this particular instance the heroic perforation of all the layers is way down in the river bed. Metaphorically, these objects are great ships that have found themselves embedded in the river bank. Something of this role is reflected in the stylisation of the tower bases themselves, by the way. As the inhabitants of this rather contemplative suburb wander over and within the meshes, they are variously planting crops, fishing, sitting above ground – or almost within it.

In a sense, it is a more cautious exploitation of the ambiguous organisation than the Shadow House, yet serves to remind me of another inspiration that has haunted me since the early 1960s, that of the reality of the three-dimensional city. It exists in the experience of subways, underpasses and the demarcation that is traditional between the ground floor and the superimposition of different functions above. Even the old Plug-in City was as much inspired by this as it was by ideas about expendability. It is intriguing to notice that the most adventurous young architects in places such as London and Los Angeles are once again designing with jutting platforms, ramps, tubes and gantries. The urge to respond to the dynamics of space are (delightfully) in the air once more. Perhaps, too, the notion of the three-dimensional city can inform the iconography of city buildings.

In the present city, all is not what it seems, as ceremonial chambers masquerade as places of real meaning whilst false ceilings are dangled within them to make them cheaper to heat. The true passages of fortune are constricted to a municipal four metres in height and we still send our lifts into the air in a feelingless, vertical dimension.

All the time, one remembers that these issues have been faced by others: the preoccupations of Marcel Duchamp's Large Glass, for instance, seem to demand of the artist as well as the spectator a radical rethinking of the language of evaluation of its icons. The question is, would Duchamp have attempted a multi-directional extension of the proposition if he had been an architect? It remains the strongest attack of the 20th century upon the relative caution and paucity of dimensionality of thought (as well as physique) of architecture. At the same time one is reminded of the parallel problems of music in having to communicate and depend from time to time upon harmonics and mathematically accurate references whilst also setting up parallel series of internalised delights. Architecture can borrow from the condition of scoring, from counterpoint, bittersweet sound and an explosion of manner at least as significant as serialisation. Can we design buildings that contain the entrails of a near-forgotten mode whilst rhetorically stating the experimentalisation of the front-line melody?

With this in mind, I have started on a primitive attempt to see what happens if one takes a few snatches of music and evaluates them as form. It is cautious as yet. The Bloch Violin Concerto was merely a group of tunes found in a book of programme notes. So far the architectural elements are imploded towers at the point of the solid note. The stave is fairly literally expressed as a series of road lanes and the space between is a park. So far the deliberate staging of the thing from a simple solidification to a more atmospheric 'architectural' image of a city serves to remind me that total consistency of interpretation rapidly reduces the creative usefulness of the thing.

PETER COOK

1936 Born Southend-on-Sea, Essex
1953-6 Bournemouth College of Art,
Department of Architecture
1958-60 Studied at the Architectural
Association, London, under James Gowan,
Peter Chamberlain, John Voelcker, John
Killick, Peter Smithson, Arthur Korn
1960-62 Worked in the office of James Cubitt
and Partners, London
1961 First issue of *Archigram* (eight issues
produced subsequently at intervals of
approximately one year)
1962 Joined 'Taylor Woodrow Design Group'
set up by Theo Crosby
1968-76 'Archigram Architects', loosely
formed in 1962, became formalised as a
group
1976- In practice in London with Christine
Hawley

Academic Positions
1964 First appointment as Assistant 5th Year
Master, Architectural Association, London.
(He has been teaching at the AA continuously ever since, as well as undertaking
teaching appointments internationally, on
loan or sabbatical from the AA,
Staedelschule, or Bartlett)
1984 Appointed Head of Department of
Architecture and Professor of Architecture at
the HbK 'Staedelschule' Frankfurt. Elected
Prorektor 1986 Re-elected and appointed
Life Professor in 1988. Sole responsibility for
small, entirely Post-Graduate School
Currently Professor of Architecture and Head
of Architecture Section at Bartlett School of
the Built Environment, University College,
London

Selected Archigram Projects 1962-76
Montreal Tower, 1963; Plug-in City, 1964;
House for 1990, 1966 (constructed inside
Harrods, Knightsbridge); Control & Choice
(represented UK at Paris Biennale 1967);
Instant City, 1968; Urban Mark, 1972

Individual Projects since 1976
Arcadia City, 1976-8; Bloch City, 1983;
Towers for Oslo, Brisbane, London, and
Frankfurt, 1984; Layer City, Kawasaki
Information City, 1986; Real City, Frankfurt,
1986; Way Out West Berlin, 1988; Rotating
House & Vertical Garden, Paris, 1989

Joint Cook and Hawley Projects
Roosevelt Island Housing, 1975 (with Ron
Herron, Ingrid Morris, Tom Heneghan, Keith
Priest, Penny Richards, John Robins, Gerry
Whale & Frank Newby); Shinkenchiku 'House
at an Intersection', 1975; Via Appia House,
1976; South Stuttgart Study, 1978; Trondheim
City Library, 1977; Speed and Information
Pavilion, Linz, 1980; Shadow House, 1981;
'Karmeliter' Museum, 1981; 'DOM' Headquar-
ters, 1981 (with Ron Herron); Landstuhl Solar
Houses, 1982; Hoechst Sports Hall, 1985;
Langen Glass Museum, 1986; Staedel
Museum extension, Frankfurt; Hamburg
riverside (first project with Christine Hawley
and Ron Herron, 1985, second project, 1987)
Housing at Lutzowplatz, Berlin, (for IBA),
1989; Pavilion for 'EXPO 90', Osaka; Canteen
block HbK, Frankfurt, 1989-92; Experimental
Over-50s housing/workshops for Edinburgh
City (planning stage)

Books and Special Editions on or by Peter Cook
Architecture-Action and Plan, Studio Vista/
Reinhold, 1967, (reprinted in Tokyo and Italy
1969); *Archigram*, Studio Vista, 1975 (reprinted 1990); *'Melting Architecture', The
work of Cook & Hawley*, Butterworth Architecture, London, 1976; Cook and Hawley
Special edition, *A+U*, Tokyo, 1981; '21 Years
– 21 Ideas', *Folio VI*, Architectural Association, London, 1985; Cook and Hawley Special
feature, *El Croquis*, July 1989; 'Peter Cook',
Extra Edition, *A+U*, 1989; *Peter Cook:
Conversations*, Art Random series: Kyoto
Shoin International (Kyoto), 1990; *New Spirit
in Architecture*, Peter Cook & Rosie Llewellyn-
Jones, Rizzoli, NY, 1991

Other Publications
'Archigram', Claude Parent, *Architecture
d'Aujourd'hui*, Paris, 1965; *Architects'
Yearbook 11*, Elek, London, 1965;
'Archigram', (special feature), *Architectural
Design*, London, 1971; 'The Work of
Archigram', *Russian Architect*, Leningrad,
1972; 'Megastructures', Reyner Banham,
Thames & Hudson, London, 1976; 'A Green-
Obsessed Architect', Arata Isozaki, *SD*,
Tokyo, 1977; 'Peter Cook', Deyan Sudjic,
Architects' Journal, London, 1978; 'Cook and
Hawley' in 'British Architecture', special issue

of *Architectural Design*, London, 1980; 'Cook,
Hawley, Herron', catalogue, Aedes Gallery,
Berlin, 1981; *Neue Architektur Darstellung*, H
Jacoby, Hatje, Stuttgart, 1981; 'Inventionen',
catalogue, Hannover Kunstverein, Hanover,
1982; *British Architecture*, Academy, London/
St Martin's Press, New York, 1982; 'Stadt und
Utopie', catalogue, Frolich und Kaufmann,
Berlin, 1982; *Spirit & Invention* (ed Peter
Cook), Architectural Association, London,
1982; *Follies*, BJ Archer, Rizzoli, New York,
1983; *Encyclopaedia of 20th Century
Architecture*, Thames & Hudson, London,
1986; 'Cook's Chef d'Oeuvre', Nigel Coates,
Architectural Review, London, 1984;
Jahrbuch für Architektur, DAM, Viewig,
Braunschweig, 1984; 'Peter Cook: Tower
Projects', catalogue, Ray Hughes Gallery,
Brisbane, 1984; *Contemporary Landscape*,
National Museum of Art, Kyoto, 1985; 'Cook &
Hawley: Langen Museum', catalogue, Aedes
Gallery, Berlin, 1986; 'Staedelschule' (Peter
Cook's master class), catalogue, Aedes
Gallery, Berlin, 1986; *Vision der Moderne*,
DAM, Frankfurt, 1986; 'Internationale
Bauausstellung Berlin' (IBA), DAM, Frankfurt,
1986; *SKALA* Interview with Peter Cook,
Copenhagen, 1986; 'Cook and Hawley:
Langen Museum', *Domus*, Milan, December
1989; *Experimental Architecture*, Princeton
Press/Aedes, 1990; *Violated Perfection*,
Aaron Betsky, Rizzoli, New York, 1990; 'Yatai:
Moveable Architecture', catalogue, Uni Co,
Nagoya, 1990; *The teacher learns from his
students*, Hauser Verlag, Darmstadt, 1990;
Architecture Now, Architecture and Natura
Press, Amsterdam, 1991; *Experimentelle
Architektur der Gegenwart*, Christian
Thomsen, Du Mont, Köln, 1991; 'Modern
Pluralism' (features Peter Cook's Inaugural
Lecture as Bartlett Professor), *Architectural
Design*, January/February 1992; *Contempo-
rary Architect Exhibition*, ed Kisho Kurokawa,
Nara, 1992; *A Decade of the RIBA Student
Competition*, UIA/Academy Editions, London,
1992; 'The Crack in the Door', *Fenster Für
Architektur*, Hauser, Darmstadt, 1992; 'An
Architecture of Optimism', Major statement
article, *Domus*, Milan, November, 1992